THEY SAID
TERMINAL

GOD SAID LIFE

THEY SAID
TERMINAL

GOD SAID LIFE

SHAWN RUSSELL

First paperback edition January 2020

Book design by Tobi Carter
Cover design by Daryl Malingin, Infinite Sign

978-1-7332475-0-4 (paperback)
978-1-7332475-1-1 (hardback)
978-1-7332475-2-8 (EPUB)
978-1-7332475-3-5 (MOBI)

Library of Congress Control Number: 2019909120

www.godsaidlife.com

Acknowledgments

I would like to first and foremost thank GOD for the loving and merciful way he carried Stephanie and I through the greatest trial of our lives.

I want to thank our faith community at Life Center for their wholehearted support and dedication to creating an environment of faith.

Thank you to our families for their support every step of the journey. Thank you, Mom, for your boldness.

Thank you to our prayer warrior team, I truly felt I was the man being let down through the roof and laid at Jesus' feet.

Thank you to the song writers who captured GOD's heart; your songs ministered deeply to me in my darkest days.

Thank you, Steve, for fully embracing a life of giving and storing up treasures in heaven.

Table of Contents

Foreword

Have you ever wondered why bad things happen to good people? Well, in *They Said Terminal (God Said Life)*, you will not find a cliché answer. What you will discover is a man with the heart of a warrior and a woman with the spirit of a champion. You will witness a husband and wife battle a death sentence with a love and strength that is nothing short of breathtaking. You will be inspired by a couple who surrounds themselves with a community of faith and who stir up hope within every human being they come in contact with. Why do bad things happen to good people? I still don't have a simple answer. But in, *They Said Terminal (God Said Life)*, you will be energized by good people overcoming bad things.

— *John Goodyear*

The Storm

L ittle did I know a storm was brewing, it would soon rattle me to the core. Fear and death were advancing, their plan was to take me out. I was forty-three years old and living a decent life by most standards. I had a respectable career, a lovely home, wonderful wife, two young adult children, a cat, and a dog. I had become a creature of habit. I no longer held many dreams for the future. I desired to survive the drudgery of life and perhaps enjoy some moments along the way. I loved my wife, children, family, and friends. I approached the world very pragmatically and by most measurements, I should have been happy, but something was missing for some time. What was missing? I had grown increasingly passive in my relationship with GOD and I truly believed I had no genuine life purpose. The season I was now crossing into was one I would wish for no one, but it was also a treasure that came wrapped in darkness. This book will enable you to experience our journey. There is sadness, pain, hope, love, joy, revelations, and miracles.

For several weeks, the pain had steadily increased. It started out as a dull pain in my lower back, I associated it with forgetting I was not in my twenties anymore. The pain continued to intensify almost daily. I supposed the torment could even be stress related. Stephanie my wife of twenty-three years and I were making frequent journeys to the hospital to be with her father Steve. We also needed to push onward with our normal workday regimens. I was convinced the agony would eventually vanish. Instead of fading away, the discomfort grew. It reached a point I could not even find a position to sleep soundly through the night. The pain was so severe I could not climb into my car without wincing. I eventually agreed with Stephanie; I needed to visit the doctor.

The family doctor started with normal inquiries. He then proceeded with pokes and prods trying to determine what could be distressing me. When a diagnosis was not clear, he decided I needed a CT scan. After following his advice and scheduling the appointment for the CT scan, I surprisingly began to feel the pain subside a bit. I believed I must be getting better.

A few days later as I was sitting in the parking lot of the imaging facility, I received a phone call from my mother. *"Shawn, I feel like God is telling me, this is not unto death!"*

"OK, mom …I am sure it will all be fine, I have been feeling much better."

Inside I pondered not unto death? Wow, that is a bit extreme; I would never have imagined death even a possibility. I was confident it was a pulled muscle or a disc in my back.

I flopped into the waiting room chair and began staring at the thirty-year-old art when my wife Stephanie called. I expressed I was feeling much better and debating if I should skip out on the scan. Why would I want to pay $1,500 to be told I am fine or had a pulled muscle nothing more? Stephanie wisely recommended I remain to be assured everything was fine. I conceded, and the CT scan was completed.

That same afternoon I already had the follow-up appointment set to interpret the CT scans. At the family doctor's office, I was ushered back to the patient room and commenced waiting. Time moved sluggishly. I wonder what was taking so long. I would love to get the word everything is fine, so I can head home. My son and his fiancée are joining us for dinner tonight and I would rather be home. After the longer than normal wait, the doctor opened the door. I instantly was alerted to the distress in his face recognizing something was up. *"Where is Stephanie?"* My stomach flip-flopped.

"She is at work."

The doctor asked if she could come to the office or join us on the phone, my pulse began to race, and the room began to spin. What could be so difficult I needed her with me? We failed to contact her on the phone, so I pleaded, "What's going on, Doc?"

"It's not good Shawn, the CT scan shows a problem! It appears that you have cancer with bone metastases."

Our family doctor is a Christian. After counseling I need to be referred to an oncologist and radiologist, we prayed together. The lab staff drew some blood to process my PSA number. (A blood marker associated with prostate cancer, Prostate Specific Antigen) I never had a PSA test or even heard of it before. I learned testing typically begins around age 50, I was only 43. How can this be happening?

I pulled into the garage sick to my stomach. My thoughts racing back and forth between I will be OK, and this is going to take me. I cried out to GOD for mercy and pleaded I want to live. I love life; I am not anxious to escape this world for the next. I want to grow old, and I want to experience my children raising their children, and I relish so many experiences this world offers.

I stumbled into the kitchen and there were my son and his fian-cée, they had already arrived for our evening plans. Not only were they here, but they arrived earlier in the day. As a gift for Mother's Day, they constructed a fire pit for Stephanie in our backyard. I did not even try to keep the news concealed. I knew my expression was a give-a-way. I laid out the bad news, and they were at a loss for words.

13

Stephanie called me on her drive home from work seeing she had missed many calls. I told her to come home, and we could have a heart-to-heart, she insisted on knowing, so I laid out the C word. We both sobbed. Stephanie believed for life from that very moment.

Stephanie arrived home. All I could contemplate was her well-being if I was soon to be taken from this world. I started explaining our life insurance and how to handle existing financial obligations. Stephanie would need to manage everything, if the worst was to quickly become a reality. She listened, but I was articulating a future neither of us desired to entertain.

We attempted to go out to dinner as previously planned, but we could not eat. Our hearts were in deep despair. We drove home, and my family came over. They dropped everything to be with us. My Mom and Dad prayed for us. They lingered most of the evening. They were attempting to comfort us while dealing with their own shock and fears.

Fears filled my imagination; would I end up bedridden soon? Would my family lose their home due to financial changes? Am I going to die? So many thoughts, I had no control of the future.

I have an inquisitive mind and I research everything that grabs my curiosity, or I want to learn about. In fact, this is so much who I am; some of our friends playfully call me "Googely Bear". This normally enlightening trait was waging war against my faith. I read and read and read. I found bad news, negative five-year survival numbers and a myriad of discouraging stories. I was searching for hope in the wrong place.

With overwhelming emotional agony late this Friday night, I typed out an email to share the grim news with one of the owners at my work. He asked how I wanted to handle the information. Should it remain as private as possible?

I stated, *"No I want everyone to know, so they can hold me up in prayer and understand if I seem off at work."* The news spread quickly about the giant I was facing. I felt like I had been air-dropped into the valley of the shadow of death.

On my way to work early Monday morning, I was crying out to GOD for mercy. As I peered through my car window, I was grasping life so differently than just a few days earlier. As I poured my heart out to GOD, I noticed a local health insurance company's billboard. Its tag line read, "Live Fearless". I thought, right, how? I read the next billboard's tagline. It was for a local college, "You will see." The very next billboard was an electronic billboard that cycles through ads. Its ad was for a car dealership using a tag line "It's easy." Live Fearless, you will see, It's Easy! Wow, GOD is this for me or am I crazy? Did I read that? It sure seems like a message just for me.

I was slumped in my office chair trying to make it through the day. My cell phone rang. It was the family doctor's office with the PSA results confirming cancer. My PSA was 24. I closed my office door and wept. *"I don't know what to do God, is it my time?"*

Overwhelming support, prayers, and encouragement began to flow as people learned the news. This included comfort from my co-workers. Many of my co-workers encouraged my faith. The support went to the highest levels of the company. In fact, they held a day of prayer for me in a secular place of business! Employees filled one of our conference rooms and lifted me before GOD, asking for healing.

Through my work, I have a benefit that provides me access to a nurse advocate to assist with any serious diagnosis. I phoned the service and connected with an advocate named Elizabeth. She worked in oncology for many years. Elizabeth explained it was unusual for a man of my age to be diagnosed with advanced prostate cancer. She believed I would be best cared for in a world-class research facility like Johns Hopkins or the Mayo Clinic. I agreed. I wanted the best possible care. I asked her to attempt to get me into Hopkins. Elizabeth shared she had connections to the multifaceted coordinator at Hopkins and she would work with her to get me in. However, in the meantime, she advised I should continue setting up the local team.

Elizabeth played an enormous part in one of the first miracles on our journey. It is my understanding it can take many months to get an appointment at a world-class facility. Elizabeth's friend at Hopkins walked my CT scans and reports over to one of the top Urologists in the world. She asked him as a favor if he would make room for me.

The doctor looked over the scans and agreed, *"Yes, he needs to be here. In his situation, we need to move him straight to biopsies."*

I was provided an appointment a mere two weeks out not months. Elizabeth told me to continue setting up local team members in case Hopkins utilized them as part of the overall care plan. I was to follow through with my already scheduled visits with the local oncologist and radiologist.

In the evening my sister Anna and her children showed up for a visit. They brought beautiful gifts. The gifts were posters with words of life and hope to plaster our kitchen cabinets. As an extra gift, she had blue rubber bracelets made that read "Pray for Shawn" on one side. On the opposite side, they read "The Glorious Unfolding." The Glorious Unfolding is a song from Steven Curtis Chapman that my sister heard on the radio shortly after my diagnosis. This song spoke to her heart as being for me. Wow was she right, this song stirred my faith. For several weeks, I would listen to it every morning. This was the first of several songs GOD used to touch my heart in deeply personal ways.

Stephanie and I remained vulnerable with one another about what we felt and the mountain we were facing. We prayed and prayed and prayed. We decided we were going to lean on GOD and do everything we could in our strength to improve my outcome. Our efforts included many components. One of the foremost was radically changing my diet to incorporate only foods that promote the best possible health. I would start journaling each day. I would write what was happening in our lives, the good, bad, horrible or mundane. We would search out the best care. We would be transparent with others about our journey and receive their help and support. I would get stress under control. I would no longer carry such heavy burdens from work. I would no longer keep attempting to "fix" our young adult daughter. In spite of the fact, she continued jumping head first into darkness and danger. I would exercise more. Most importantly we would seek GOD daily and spend time in the word and in praise and worship. We would also limit negative inputs to our minds. One of the giant ones was the news. I had been quite the news junky. This transformation included television programs and movies that did not encourage our spirits. Our understanding and the depth of these changes would evolve throughout our journey as GOD revealed more to our hearts.

Local Oncologist Day... Dr. Death

We were about to be introduced to the local oncologist. It was a dark but enlightening day. Stephanie and I grabbed chairs in the examination room waiting on the doctor. We were incredibly nervous but had hope. The doctor entered the room. He did not carry a friendly demeanor or countenance. He questioned why we were visiting him. I clarified we were setting up a local team of specialists. We foresaw these specialists may partner with Johns Hopkins as the lead on my care if appropriate.

The doctor said, *"That is doable, but this is a difficult diagnosis and I will explain why."*

In the office stood a whiteboard, the doctor preceded to discuss the diagnosis and how there is no cure. *"I won't bu**sh*t you."* He blurted. *"The best we can do is give you some time."*

The doctor proceeded to scribble drug names on his whiteboard along with how long they slow or limit cancer growth. To our disbelief, he would not permit me to interrupt his presentation to ask questions. Once he had the list of drugs and duration they may work on the whiteboard I saw he was granting me about a year and a half to three years maximum to live. I sensed I was about to pass out from anxiety but found the strength to verbalize my first question.

"Would how I eat improve my projected outcome and would changing my lifestyle help?"

With an absolute indignant tone, the doctor mouthed, *"Eat whatever you want it won't matter!"* He apparently observed the dread in my face and that I was faint. He offered me a Coke?!?! I refused and could not find the strength to articulate most of the questions I had hoped to ask.

I concluded, *"Hopkins will be the lead on my care, and once they set a treatment plan in motion we will get rolling. If the plan includes me getting Chemotherapy locally, I will be in touch."*

The horrible prognosis and way he presented no hope crushed our hearts on the drive home. Stephanie and I discussed how we felt. We appreciate that GOD's word declares there is power of life and death in the tongue. We are speaking and believing for life. We most certainly need a healthcare team that speaks life and has hope. We decided we would never return to see this doctor even if we need a local oncologist. I spoke to our nurse advocate Elizabeth and asked if she could find us a more positive local oncologist for the team.

This day was difficult and wounded our souls, however, it motivated us to surround ourselves with words of life. This included people who would speak life! Even though this doctor declared my final countdown had started ticking. We would count upwards and revel in the blessing of each day GOD had for us. Stephanie employed her gift to write. She began providing updates to our closest prayer warriors almost daily. These updates included everything. Our sorrows, hopes, encouraging words and messages GOD sent our way and even news of divinely ordered scenarios. Stephanie's writings were critically significant. They conveyed our need to those supporting us in prayer.

We were determined to place our confidence in GOD. I began using my gift to research, now looking for things that would offer hope; educate me on nutrition or accounts of people who beat the odds. I would occasionally stumble into subjects or articles that tripped me into fear and sadness. I gradually became better at deciding what to read and what to bypass.

On Mother's Day morning, I arose early unable to sleep. I yearned for the perfect outcome and needed to understand what I could do as a steward of my body to make it through this. I focused on stories of miraculous outcomes of others diagnosed with stage 4 cancers and their journeys. Each account gave me hope this did not have to be a death sentence, some people do win. I knew my hope needed to be centered in GOD, but that he also provides us wisdom. That wisdom could play a part in my journey. I was amazed that I noticed certain commonalities in the success stories. A few of these commonalities were: patients radically changed their diets, almost all would both speak and visualize positive outcomes in their own bodies, many would focus on releasing stress and negative elements from their lives.

I was going to replicate some of these commonalities and merge them into my life. I began by praying that GOD helps me absorb what I am learning from these stories. I created visualizations for my body that I promised myself I would picture each day. My personal visualization in its early stage included a few parts and looked like this. 1) My white blood cells and NK or natural killer cells looked like giant Pac-man. These Pac-men knew exactly where cancer cells were hiding. They would gobble them up. In my mind, I imagined the cancer cells as tiny and feeble. 2) For my bones, I imagined a flaming finger targeting and searing cancer out, while iron barricades surrounded my bones and kept cancer from being able to spread. 3) I imagined my lymph nodes being surrounded by impenetrable casings that prevented any cancer cells being loosed. 4) I would envision the PSA number I was given as a degree on a thermometer that kept plummeting towards zero. 5) I imagined any cancer cells freely traveling in my blood being captured and put in prison cells until a Pac-man destroyed them. I used these visualizations for quite some time whenever I thought about cancer and as I would attempt to fall asleep at night.

Stephanie roused on that Mother's Day morning, and I revealed my strategy for visualizations as we prepared for church. I could not wait to arrive at church, I so thirsted for prayers. We belong to a remarkable fellowship; Life Center in Harrisburg, Pennsylvania. Our church body embraces the intimate, loving, and omnipotent GOD who created all that is and commands everything that is or will ever be. I knew I would be presented with words of life.

We arrived at church and the moment anyone who knew what we were facing met eyes with us; they came over to pray and encourage us. Anne Stock, the wife of our senior pastor, voiced prayers that strengthened us with hopeful visions. She exclaimed, *"I can see you holding a newborn grandchild; I can see you with your beloved dog Zeek and he is an old dog, I can see you at a future anniversary together on the beach."* Anne also spurred us to celebrate the victories along the way, even the minor ones. Several people proclaimed that we will come through this and there will be a book in the future. Others promised they would carry us in prayer the entire journey and not relent until we see the victory. Women would grasp Stephanie's hands and say, *"He's got this, and you got this."*

A gathering including my family prayed after the service. My father pictured cancer collapsing in on itself until nothingness. My brother sincerely felt to speak calm over us. After prayer, we were asked what we sensed while being prayed for. Stephanie mentioned she discerned, *"This is not a battle, not a war and that we were to rest, God fights for us."*

I pronounced, *"When we were praying I could already imagine a time where I am through this and helping encourage others giving them hope on their journeys."*

Anne again spoke to us after the prayer circle let up and whispered, *"I want you to know, each time I hear someone has found out about what you are facing, they all seem to have the same response. They can't wait to hear the story of what God has done for you! And many alleged we were a handpicked couple to carry something God is doing."*

While the prayer time was amazing. My spirit was so parched; I could have lingered there until my healing was manifested. Stephanie and I both appreciate the power in prayer. We would saturate ourselves in it, accepting it from as many as were willing to call out our names to GOD.

Treasure from
the Darkness

The tongue has the power of life and death; speak life.

Treasure in Heaven

One of Stephanie's writings during our journey is below. Only three weeks before my diagnosis her father Steve was entering heaven. Understanding a bit more about Steve captured by her writing will include you in a revelation that Stephanie had shortly after his passing that is paramount to our story.

Treasures My Dad Planted

I managed to crawl into bed this time instead of waking up on the couch. My head swirling with our recent news of Shawn's diagnosis, racing thoughts of just burying my Dad two weeks prior to Shawn's diagnosis, and our son embarking on his first deployment with the Air Force to the Middle East. My heart too heavy for the pillow, too heavy for my covers, just too heavy. I felt like the men I loved were leaving me and packing their bags in a sense and never coming back one by one.

Dad was in Heaven and I was still processing his quick parting after being sick with an infection in his body for about 3 weeks. My dad, Stephen, was injured in a forklift accident 36 years prior and won a money settlement. He almost died and became a paraplegic. His whole life changed. A tragedy. During that time, my dad grew close to the LORD. I witnessed his childlike faith in action as he gave to churches, ministries, to the poor, family, friends, and there is too much to write how he gave. When my dad passed away he only had $80 left in the bank. I only have a sweatshirt that he wore to remember him by. There was no earthly inheritance.

All these thoughts racing through my head as I drifted off to sleep. Sometime during the night, I woke up and started praying for Shawn again. Suddenly, I heard in my spirit, *"You got it all wrong. He did leave you something, an inheritance. A very wealthy one in heaven. He planted for 36 years of faith, healing, and miracles. You are heir to this inheritance. It's yours! No man on earth can take it from you. No demon can lie to you about it. The treasure is protected in heaven."*

The next morning, I shared with Shawn the revelation that came to me in the middle of the night. This sprung up deep emotions and I began to sob before the LORD. In prayer, I asked the book-keepers in Heaven to look up my Father's name. I was shouting, screaming, sobbing, and calling down my inheritance. I was the rightful heir to the treasure that was hidden there. I reminded the book-keepers what was exactly planted there. I was out of breath by the time I was done in prayer calling down the inheritance.

I made a withdrawal of *faith* for exactly what it was planted for *healing* and *miracles*. I received the best inheritance ever, a heavenly one that moves mountains, that heals, that *glory* unfolds, and *miracles* take place at every turn. A supernatural dimension that I inherited. Every time I remember what my dad did those 36 years, I feel incredibly loved and close to him. The fields are producing a harvest now. It's time to work those fields and watch *healing* and *miracles* take place. The first one being Shawn. I feel at times, that my Dad saved his life.

This is His

Our son Josiah was nearing takeoff for his first deployment to the Middle East. Our hearts were now calling out for his safe return. The deployment would be briefer than most. Only three months, but with so many unknowns about my health and the danger he would confront it was a burdensome time.

My first appointment at Hopkins for biopsies was on the calendar. I still had a few local appointments including a full body bone scan in the coming days. My thought life was a roller coaster during these two weeks. At times I would be oppressed by the fear of the worst. I would weep uncontrollably. At other moments, I would receive a phone call, email, text or visit that would comfort my spirit and steer me back to a place of trust in GOD. I felt loved by so many.

My mother lovingly prepared us wholesome organic meals. She would find ways to incorporate ingredients with powerful cancer-fighting properties. My nephew showed up and mowed our grass. A nurse friend who knew I was researching foods and natural ways to help my body sent me an article. The article highlighted watercress and by what method it impedes metastasis in cancer. This article was very beneficial because it assisted me in setting a course on the quality of research and type of resources to evaluate. I would consult similar studies of natural foods that impact cancer, boost the immune system, increased white blood cells and improve prostate health. I determined I would keep researching and learning but focus on scholarly articles. This research would continue throughout my journey, and I would improve my protocol any time I understood more. I would pray about my nutritional decisions and asked GOD to offer me peace about the appropriate choices for me.

I devoted time to reading scriptures on healing and soaking in worship music. My heart longed to simply reach out and touch the hem of his garment. My father suggested I go to the "healing room" at church. I was not aware, but in our prayer room at church, a window of time weekly was dedicated to praying specifically for healing. I agreed, I was decidedly going to make time to be there despite the fact it would require taking time from work.

I arrived for the healing room session. I was not certain what to expect. They had a very sensible way of praying. I completed a questionnaire with some basic information about myself and what I needed prayer for. This form was taken into the prayer room where those praying for the sick were already in a place of worship. They prayed over the request and person needing prayer. I was called into the room and sensed it was holy ground. I shared more detail about the diagnosis and the condition of my heart. I sobbed tears of desperation. Many miraculous prayers and words of faith were declared over me. My spirit leaped as it agreed with the prayers for my healing. Oh, the power of words yet again!

Saturday morning came; Stephanie and I decided to visit her grandmother and aunt who live together. We sought to visit and express gratitude for their prayers. Jill, my wife's aunt, shared her expectation was to see a miracle in my life. She proceeded to recall times in her life when she experienced GOD move in very personal and miraculous ways. My wife's grandmother who we affectionately call Nanan declared we would be "tellers", that we would be victorious and share with others what GOD has done. After she had shared, I had an impression n my heart and uttered with my mouth *"God loves grandmother prayers; they have a special place in his heart."* In that moment I reflected on how grandmothers endured many years, beheld many trials and frequently possessed deep prayer lives. Stephanie and I were very encouraged. We decided to end our evening watching the movie "The War Room". Such a mighty praying grandmother is in this story for sure.

It was Sunday again. I could not wait to arrive at church. Once more I was covered by prayers. Certain words from a prayer stuck with me enough to journal them. *"Be persistent in your prayers before God, Speak Life and hold onto his promises."* My parents again visited bearing a gift. They purchased a book written by a local pastor Dave Hess. Dave had confronted dire odds and near-death experiences with cancer, however, GOD healed him. I could not wait to devour his story and learn what GOD did for Dave. I so ached for GOD to move in the miraculous for me too. I read the entire book in one evening.

Dave's story was hopeful but also triggered a fear to surface. I did not desire to be on deaths doorstep before receiving healing. I pondered, could my faith endure that pressure, or would I fall into despair? Would I simply accept it was my time? At this point, I was not sure.

Day and night, I was calling out to GOD. I would ask him to clearly communicate with me, grant me dreams, revelations, angelic visits or anything my depleted spirit could cling onto. I retired to bed this evening and once more pleaded to understand GOD's heart for me. I dozed off and fell into a dream. I was in a small room reminiscent of a cabin or a mobile home. With me was a young girl but certainly not a delightful one. This girl mirrored someone from a horror movie. She attacked me. I struggled and wrestled with her. I had the power to subdue her, pinning her to the ground. Believing the attack was one of but a foolish child, I released her expecting the fight to end. However, she was resolved to destroy me. The cycle of attack and release repeated. Many times, I bested her, holding her down securely then releasing, only to have her attack again. My adversary's power seemed to increase with subsequent skirmishes. I analyzed my surroundings for alternatives. I perceived at some point, I would no longer maintain the advantage. Soon I would be overtaken. Suddenly in my spirit, while still dreaming I had a revelation. I must not continue battling her in this fashion. Her strength would indeed continue to increase. I was to forcefully remove her from the building altogether.

I woke up and processed my dream. My heart exposed the truth. This girl represented fear. The reality was, I was staring down fear and aspiring to subdue it with rational thinking. At times this would impart short bursts of peace, but I always returned to fear. Is GOD reminding me I must not wrestle the spirit of fear but kick it out my mind? The answer must be yes. Fear does not originate from GOD. I appealed to GOD for assistance. Then in courage, I rebuked fear from my life.

I would only have one more sunrise before the biopsy procedure. I made the decision not to venture to work. Alternatively, I needed a day of reflection, worship, and prayer. A great number of messages sharing how I was included on prayer lists and on hearts flooded my phone. I parked myself in worship and maintained my thoughts on GOD. I sensed with confidence that GOD had a plan for my life that included healing. I so wanted to capture the feelings of this moment with the ability to relive it on demand. I did not want to revisit fear. Stephanie arrived home from work and we packed for our trip to Baltimore. We would spend the night near the hospital awaiting the early appointment. My brother James volunteered to join us and play chauffeur, considering I might not be able to drive post biopsies.

We entered Inner Harbor, Baltimore. This was ordinarily a setting I enjoyed. In the past, it included strolls with Stephanie, romantic dinners and time away from home. Tonight, I could not delight in anything. Unfortunately, I was once more allowing fear to torment my soul.

We retired for the night. In the darkness of the night, I pleaded over and over *"God please let me know your heart. Help me understand what is happening."*

I could not sleep well. I tossed and turned waking repeatedly to gaze at the clock. Most of the night, I had no dreams, angelic visitation or revelations of any sort. I drifted to sleep after a 3 am awakening. Only two hours of possible rest remained. In the moments before the alarm was about to sound off, I had a dream or vision, or some combination of the two. It was but one word. I visualized the word *"THIS"* directly before my eyes. My soul was compelled to read this heaven-sent message. As I looked fixedly at the word, I saw it no longer as one word. I viewed the word *this* as three words simultaneously inside a word. *This is His!* My heart surged inside my chest. GOD, is this you or a comforting angel? Are angels ministering peace to me? Is this battle yours and I need not fear? I did not have the answers. I did however, experience a release of stress and new hope. Stephanie awoke, and I shared my experience. Our courage to face the day increased.

Biopsies at Hopkins Day (May 24, 2017)

This first visit to Hopkins was a whirlwind of emotions. I received the vision that "this is his" but anxiety was clawing at me. Hopkins is an amazing facility. It was grander than any hospital I had ever set foot in before. The closest comparison is a bustling airport only healthcare. There were patients from all over the world arriving here for care. My Hopkins team would collect and process biopsies of my cells to customize a treatment plan. Using these biopsies, they would better grasp the pathology of the cancer.

Stephanie, James and I all had a seat in the waiting room, knowing soon my name would be called. Stephanie was texting, keeping prayer warriors updated. My name was shouted, and I was escorted to an examination room. The nurse instructed me to disrobe and put on a gown. The nurse left the room for a few moments and I prayed. I sized up the room and noticed a computer station. Above the monitor was a picture. I got up to take a closer look. This picture was printed out and certainly not the quality of the other artwork in the hospital. This wall hanging was divinely here for me. The image was of a man receiving surgery. Around the patient was a team of doctors and nurses. Standing near the chief surgeon observing and guiding was Jesus! My soul soared with hope. I quickly located my phone snapped an image to share later.

I put my phone away and the door opened. The nurse followed by nine other people flooded the room. I was quite shocked, and it was evident on my face. The head doctor strolled in a few moments later and began to speak with me. He shared who everyone was. The entourage included multiple doctors, nurses, and residents in training for good measure. I was asked if it was OK for the residents to stay. I mumbled, *"Yes, I just appreciate Hopkins getting me in and for the help, I believe you are going to offer me." I could not maintain my tongue I whimpered, "Is there hope for me?"*

The chief doctor fielded the question: *"Yes there is hope and breakthroughs all the time. I am glad it is 2017 and not 1997."*

I won't sugarcoat the details of the biopsy. The procedure was extremely painful and difficult to endure. Finally, the doctor concluded my personal torture session. He explained, *"Hopkins will contact you in a couple of days to discuss the next steps for treatment."*

After the bleeding had stopped, I managed to clothe myself and return to the waiting room. I acquired a small limp from the pain. I appreciated the fact my brother would be driving us home. I shared the experience with Stephanie and James showing them the photo. I joked about ticket stubs to watch the show and the final count for the crowd in attendance. Knowing my brother's humor, a bit, I made another joke. Using my water bottle as a prop, I illustrated the probe size and entry point I endured.

In an elevator, as we made our way to leave the hospital, Steph spoke softly to me, *"You did great today."*

I whispered, *"I did well today, but this is only the beginning."*

We were now in this elevator along with an older woman possibly a grandma. She was using a cane to support her walking efforts. I knew she overheard our whispers. Perhaps she was a fellow follower of Christ or even an angel incognito. She turned to me as the elevator door opened and declared with boldness. *"I don't know what you're going through, but you will come through it! Take that, I am giving you my blessing today!"* I could barely utter the words *thank you* as she exited the elevator.

We made it back to our vehicle and I laid down for the journey home. Stephanie updated friends, family and prayer warriors on how the day unfolded. My heart longed silently, *Please let the biopsies show no cancer and this whole thing is somehow a big mistake.*

Treasure from
the Darkness

*God knows our weakness, our sorrow, our pain, and our
suffering. He is not surprised, and he is compassionate. Give
yourself room to be real with your feelings.*

Up & Down

I required a few days to heal post biopsies. Many hours of my time were invested in searching my heart. One evening, Stephanie and I watched *The Shack*. The manner in which this story personifies GOD's love for all his children and how he is particularly fond of us ministered to me.

I reflected on my temperament towards my daughter Ashley. Our current relationship and her life choices troubled me daily. It was a struggle in my heart from morning to night. Oh, how I wanted to do what in my mind would equate to fixing her. But alas, I cannot change anyone's heart. GOD revealed to me that I needed to unconditionally love Ashley, forgive her for the pain she has caused and believe his plan for her life. Knowing my personality of wanting to quick-fix things, I could only achieve such a heart change with GOD's help. I repented and fixed my heart and eyes towards only love for Ashley.

Friends, family, and co-workers provided encouragements daily. One sent a music video of the next song to ravish my heart. The song was "No Longer Slaves to Fear". I pondered this concept, I am a child of GOD and he loves me. Why have I permitted fear to be a dominating force in my life? I asked GOD to help me kick out fear forever and to comprehend myself as his child.

Another friend sent us a video. It was a testimony from a man diagnosed with cancer, told he would die. He received a miracle and lived. This man now spends his life ministering to others. In this video, he was being interviewed by a Christian broadcaster in front of a live audience. He announced, *"I have something I want to read to everyone."* He pulled a card out of his pocket and proceeded to read *"Dear Cancer… It's my birthday again!"* I wept instantly. He continued with his healing testimony. As powerful as it was, I was most affected by an additional story he shared. This story had taken place after his healing. He was leading a prayer team and felt GOD prompt him to have the team join him at the intensive care unit of a children's cancer hospital. He questioned GOD, *"How will we get in."* In his spirit, he heard, *"Don't worry I will give you a key."* So in faith, the group traveled to the ICU and as expected, they could not simply walk in and pray for the children. Outside a locked door was the intercom speaker. This man pushes the button and explained why they were there.

The responding party barked, *"You cannot come back here."*

This man of faith then repeated what he heard in his heart, *"But I have a key."*

The healthcare worker on the other side uttered, *"What? Hold on I'll come see your key."*

The man leading the group began praying silently, *"God you said you would give me a key, where is it, they are on their way now to the door?"* He got a revelation of what the key was.

A nurse cracked the door and demanded: *"Where's your key at?"*

This man raised his pant legs and showed his scars. He shared his healing testimony and their heart to pray for the children. The team was granted permission to pray and miracles abounded. Their group is now welcomed frequently to pray for the children. I wept at GOD's mercy and willingness to heal.

Sunday rolled around. My parents attend a sister church to ours, Christ Community. The senior pastor Dave Hess had a miracle healing from cancer and I read his book. My parents wanted him to pray for me. We joined them for their morning service. Pre-service, the pastor greeted us in the atrium and learned more about the diagnosis. He laid his hands on me and prayed. I heard him repeat the words my mother had pronounced at the beginning, *"not unto death"* and *"long life"*. My spirit soared with hope and belief GOD was promising me life. After worship, the leader who knew of my diagnosis revealed it to the congregation. The room unified in prayer for my healing. I was overwhelmed by the faith.

Memorial Day arrived, so Stephanie and I were off work. We went for a nice walk and shared our hearts. I expressed how I ached for peace that passes understanding. I was constantly teetering between faith and fear. My mind was wrestling anxiety about the results of the biopsy reports. Steph loved on me and expressed how she absolutely sees me someday as an old man and great grandfather. My heart overflowed with love for her. I so admired her faith and trust in GOD's plan. I challenged my heart to have greater trust in GOD's timetable and directions for my life.

The phone rang, the caller ID read Johns Hopkins, so I answered. I was longing to hear somehow this is a misinterpretation and there is no cancer. Instead, the doctor explained, *"Unfortunately, the cancer is confirmed, and it is aggressive, a Gleason score of 9."* His words hammered me like a spike being driven into my chest. I rationalized to myself, so not only is this cancer terrible, it's horrendous and aggressive. The urology doctor continued to advise, *"Surgery is not an option; you need to meet with the best oncologist for treating someone with your diagnosis. His name is Dr. Emmanuel Antonorakis."* Suddenly hearing the first name Emmanuel grabbed my heart and plucked it from despair. Emmanuel's literal meaning is *God with us*! Soon I was to receive a call from the scheduling department to add me on the calendar to consult with Emmanuel.

My flesh and faith were in a tug of war for dominance. I phoned Stephanie in tears and shared the difficult news. Stephanie did not waver and saw Emmanuel's name as assurance GOD was hearing prayers and moving on our behalf. Sensing the battle between my faith and fear she sent out a request for help, asking people to pray for us. I was descending into a dark place and needed to be bailed out. As much as I tried I could not shake the fear and sadness. Today fear and cancer were triumphing. I had no will power, resolve or faith to overcome the voices in my head taunting *"You will die, see how foolish you are trusting in God, you deserve to die, think of all the sins you have done in your life, God is not on your side, he is judging you."* I sobbed and permitted my mind to daydream about my family going on without me.

Another call from Hopkins came up on the caller ID. This time it was the scheduler. *"I am sorry, but we have been unable to find a time slot for you with Dr. Emmanuel. The very next opening he has is not until the very end of July. We can however set you up with another oncologist on our staff the earliest opening is June 24."*

I acknowledged, *"OK, please set the appointment for me."* Once the phone call ended, I was battered by sadness. I could not get an oncology appointment for a month and if it was to be Emmanuel not for two months. I visualized the cancer growing and running rampant in my body for another month. I attempted to self soothe, reminding myself of the meaning of the name Emmanuel and the burst of hope it gave me. Perhaps GOD let me see this name to give me hope, even though I was now being scheduled with another doctor. At this point, the voices of despair and fear were so loud in my mind I was certain I would not hear GOD even if he was using a bullhorn.

The emergency prayers triggered change. My nurse advocate Elizabeth called me and said, *"I was able to secure the visit with a better local oncologist that will be able to at least get you started on a hormone deprivation shot, they come with stellar feedback."*

Elizabeth knew how dark our previous local oncology visit had been and was very compassionate. I murmured, *"When is the visit?"*

She said, "June 13."

"Wow, that is perfect. That is one day after Stephanie and I get back from the cruise we had planned months before the diagnosis. I thought we were about to cancel, this is also sooner than Hopkins can get me in."

At least the cancer would only continue growing for a couple of weeks I thought. I asked Elizabeth a question. *"Should I just cancel the appointment I have set for tomorrow with a local radiologist since we know I need to go the oncology route?"*

Elizabeth wisely advised me to keep the appointment. She noted, *"You never know what Hopkins will recommend for treatment now or in the future and it could include radiation at some point."*

Those praying for us were sending me emails and texts with messages from their hearts. Some sharing what they were sensing from GOD. All these messages indicated GOD had a plan and it included me living. My brother James tends to be a bit reserved about his faith but shared he was driving home very late the other night but wanted to see me, almost to the point of wanting to wake me up late at night. Instead, James felt GOD's leading, *"Just go pray over his home while they sleep."* James drove to our home and walked up to the door.

He placed his hand on the door and only one word repeatedly came out of his mouth. *"Calm... Calm... Calm."* James left, not sure he would ever tell us about that night but my need for encouragement today was great.

A third phone call from Hopkins came in. The scheduler indicated a cancellation occurred for an oncologist on June 6, and they were offering me that appointment. I asked if I could call back with a decision shortly. If I accept the appointment, we must cancel our cruise. I had just experienced the excitement that we could still go. We so longed and needed some beauty and peace. Not to mention we would lose all the money spent. Canceling the cruise could however speed up getting hormone treatment by one week. I did not want to do this; it did not feel right to me. What if this was the last trip I would ever have with Stephanie? Wouldn't it be better to give her some comforting memories of me? I turned down the appointment.

Stephanie encouraged me all evening. She restated all the things GOD was doing. Emmanuel, "he is with us". Others have said you will live with boldness. Your brother spoke calm over the storm we are in. I got into one of the top hospitals in the world. We turned on some music and I eventually drifted to sleep.

Treasure from
the Darkness

*Do not venture into a massive battle alone; there
is strength in numbers. We need each other.*

The Shift

I woke up wobbly, feeling burdens from the day before. Stephanie awoke, the first words I heard were, *"Shawn did we make a mistake by not taking that appointment on June 6? I just feel you really need that shot as soon as possible."*

I uttered, *"I don't think I could even get it now if we wanted it, I am sure they called someone else and filled it."*

Stephanie agreed but reiterated she wished I could receive the shot before we left on our cruise. I had no idea how that could possibly happen.

Today I was scheduled to visit a local radiologist. I was expecting a meet and greet visit, simply securing a local radiology team if they were to be part of my care.

I arrived for my late afternoon radiologist appointment and was led back to the patient exam room. After a short wait Dr. Salinger, the local radiologist entered the room. He carried a much more comforting demeanor than the local oncologist. We had a short introduction and I explained my desire for a local partner if radiation ever becomes part of my care. Much to my surprise, Dr. Salinger advised me he reviewed all my scans and pathology reports very closely. He proceeded to educate me on the cancer, what the Gleason scores indicated and the gravity of the diagnosis. He did comfort me that breakthroughs are happening, and we are not yet talking about palliative care and hospice.

I shared my wife's impression that I needed the hormone shot as soon as possible. He agreed. I mentioned the upcoming cruise. I also let him know the dates for the new local oncologist and when the Hopkins oncologist visit would be.

In his eyes, I saw compassion. Dr. Salinger stated, *"Let's try to get that shot approved for you before you leave for your cruise in a couple of days. I know it's very late afternoon but let's try."*

It was after 5 pm, the staff was closing the office. Dr. Salinger urged his office manager to linger and attempt to reach someone at the insurance company to approve the shot for tomorrow. I was blown away by this effort to go the extra mile. Dr. Salinger also took time to complete a write-up, providing his analysis on my condition. He shared the report with my nurse advocate and faxed a copy to Hopkins. We stuck around the office for another hour and a half, but no success on the approval. I was advised to keep my phone near me; efforts would start again in the morning.

I traveled home encouraged that a doctor was willing to work so hard on my behalf. Stephanie and I sensed a shift taking place. We prayed to ask for help resolving the details around this treatment. We had no clue a radiologist could order this type of treatment. We were thankful I kept this appointment.

Stephanie shared our praise report with our prayer warrior friends. Instead of letting up, it inspired them to press in more. A handful of our friends had an impression to start fasting and praying. I wept again, this time because I experienced love. I conversed in my heart with GOD about how I have never carried anyone like I am being carried. Please make me that type of intercessor for others.

Our dear friend Libby shared something funny yet amazing that she and her husband Larry were doing for us. Every time the phone would ring with a solicitation call or unknown number they would stop and pray for me throughout the day. Thank you for friends GOD.

Amazing Day!

Everyone has had days where difficult challenges snowball. This was a day like that, but the blessing snowball kept growing. I answered the phone, Dr. Salinger's office manager exclaimed, *"We were able to get the hormone shot approved for you tomorrow."*

Tomorrow was June 2. Treatment would now be available two days before the cruise! Only a day earlier, the earliest treatment was weeks into the future. Such wonderful news, it moved Stephanie's heart deeply as she perceived this was urgent.

Medical explanation; hormone deprivation treatment blocks testosterone production in the body. This is important as it significantly slows prostate cancer's growth and spread while it remains an effective therapy. Unfortunately, for most men, it only works for a period of time before cancer cells mutate into a version no longer needing testosterone. In my situation, it would put the brakes on cancer growth until we could get to Hopkins and plan more aggressive treatment.

Another phone call, Elizabeth, my nurse advocate, saying, *"Wow that Dr. Salinger must be a very good doctor, he took the time to call me and review your scans and pathology work and send a write-up summary over to Hopkins as well."*

I voiced the good news of treatment being approved so fast. She agreed this was tremendous news.

My emotions were changing. I started imagining I may enjoy our cruise. I would no longer carry the fear that the cancer was growing and spreading during the trip. Yet again, the phone rang. It was Johns

Hopkins. The world-class urologist who completed my biopsies was in direct discussions with Dr. Emmanuel. The two concluded it was imperative I was under Dr. Emmanuel's care. Dr. Emmanuel agreed to create a special consulting appointment. The special pre-dawn appointment would be on June 14! Only two days after the cruise.

Wow! So many pieces were being divinely rearranged in our favor. We would make the cruise. I was to receive the hormone treatment earlier than anyone foresaw. I would be in the care of the top doctor, who had no availability for months. Our appointment was set only days after our cruise. My doctor's name is Emmanuel!

Gratitude overwhelmed me. Just look at what was unfolding. GOD was removing mountains and aligning circumstances surpassing anything man could do. The only appropriate response was worship and thankfulness. Stephanie and I broadcast the miracles unfolding with our friends and family. Without fail everyone saw GOD's hand at work. Even non-believers we know as friends and co-workers were inspired by our testimony. They too began speaking words of life to us, believing we were experiencing the beginnings of a miracle.

One of our precious friends Libby expounded, *"Your story is reminding me of a book I read called* When God Winks at You.*"* This book is full of stories that at first glance could appear to be coincidences but when looked at with faith clearly display GOD moving in someone's life in personal and supernatural ways. I decided during the last minute cruise shopping tomorrow, I would pick this book up to read.

I woke up expectant. I had time before my hormone deprivation shot. I decided to take things slow, enjoy my breakfast then a peaceful stroll with my dog, Zeek. After the walk, I went shopping and purchased a few items for the cruise. The most notable items were from the local Barnes and Noble. The book *When God Winks* and a journal. I knew I needed to capture everything I was experiencing. There were many amazing journals but, I felt drawn to purchase one with a picture of the *Tree of Life Surrounded by a Circle*. Yes! This is the one I thought. He is the vine and we are the branches. I would transfer the first couple weeks of my writings to my new permanent journal.

I drove to a park a short distance from the doctor's office overlooking the city of Harrisburg. On a swinging bench, I started reading the new book. Wow, these stories are amazing. GOD was touching people's hearts and meeting needs in very personal ways. How anyone could push these aside as mere coincidences is beyond me. I talked with GOD asking him to establish in me an intercessor's heart. Being supported in prayer by others had become so important to me and boosted my faith daily. I know GOD wants us to knock and keep knocking; but I understood this today differently.

The hormone treatment was a little painful, two subcutaneous shots into the stomach. Only this round of treatment would target the stomach. Apparently, there are a few medication options that block testosterone. Dr. Salinger requested this one known for lowering testosterone the quickest. Knowing these therapies usually only work for a duration of time I prayed from a desperate heart *"Please do not let my cells mutate around this treatment."* I felt my faith rise as I recalled what GOD had already orchestrated in my favor. I committed in my heart to keep returning to a place of trust and to reject fear when it whispers lies into my ears. *"Fear is a liar! God never lies. God always speaks in Love. Love casts out all Fear,"* I proclaimed. I pondered to myself if this is my time wouldn't he at least reveal it in a gentle loving way? I drove home to join Stephanie in cruise preparations.

Treasure from
the Darkness

*Open your heart and eyes to the world
around you, God is speaking.*

The Shed

June 3, 2017

Tomorrow we would set sail on our cruise. Emotions were certainly a roller coaster today. One moment I am flying high, excited about our first trip ever to the Bahamas. Moments later fear attempts to hijack my joy, whispering "this is your last vacation ever." My spirit rose up and reprimanded my brain. Remember your dream! Don't wrestle fear, kick it out! I rebuked fear and battled my mind to stop entertaining fear.

A devotional I read for the day was amazingly appropriate. It was the story of the Israelite spies being sent to scout out the promised land. Ten of the twelve came back full of fear but two, Joshua and Caleb came back declaring GOD has given us the land and it is good. The writer of the devotional explained all twelve had experienced the same land and witnessed the same giants. The only difference was how the two with courage viewed GOD. Yes, there were giants, but they knew GOD was greater than the giants. I prayed, *"Yes, Lord, cancer is a giant, but I know you are greater than cancer. Please help me not to submit to fear, etch this in my heart."*

The last of our bags were packed. Stephanie and I chose to visit her grandmother and then stop by my sister's house for an evening fire pit. When we arrived, other family was already there. We joined them around the fire and stories were shared about the growing army of people praying. My Dad revealed people regularly committing to pray for us. My Mom mentioned a lady at the grocery store asked for one of the blue bracelets to remind her to keep praying for me.

My sister-in-law Ashley shared a story that tugged at our hearts. She is a teacher and a number of her students saw her blue bracelet and inquired what it was for. She told them of my diagnosis and they said they would pray for me too. During the last day of the school year, there was an annual teacher kickball game. Students attend to cheer on their grade level teachers. Each time it was Ashley's turn to kick, her students would chant *"Do it for Shawn! Do it for Shawn!"* Compassion and support from people you may never meet are unexpected blessings.

We were about ready to call it a night when a close friend of ours, Sunny, sent a text. *"Do you know what tomorrow is? The same day you set sail on your cruise is National Cancer Survivors Day!!"* Wow, we had no idea. This cruise was booked long before the diagnosis. What an amazing "GOD Wink!" At this point, we were no longer seeing moments like this as mere coincidence. GOD was speaking to us and whispering, *"You will be a survivor, Shawn."* Stephanie and I talked about the cruise as we lay in bed. Both our hearts were expectant GOD would be close to us in the Bahamas and the escape would refresh our weary souls.

We were destined to make this cruise. Somehow amidst the whirlwind of doctor appointments and scans, this cruise, booked months earlier debarked during the only window of time we could possibly go. Not only that, our ship was leaving port on national cancer survivor's day!

While at sea I had leisure time to read, rest, and contemplate. I was able to appreciate the beauty and vastness of creation. GOD's love is deeper than the ocean. My struggle, as enormous as it appeared was puny to GOD. I simply lingered staring at the ocean and praying. I contemplated the truth I am only one person in the history of the world, on one planet that amounts to a speck of dust compared with the vastness of the universe and my life span itself was only the shortest blip of time. The cancer I was magnifying was nothing more than tiny dysfunctional cells.

Selah.

GOD, the creator of all things loves me and desires a relationship with me. GOD is conscious of my every hair and thought. Not mine alone but every one of the billions on earth. I questioned myself, why do we attempt to comprehend GOD viewed through our shortsighted lenses filtered by our limited human knowledge? Certainly, I can consider it true, for GOD it takes but a word and the cancer I dreaded would be healed. With a humbled heart, I asked the creator of all to have mercy and if he might be glorified by healing me.

Stephanie and I reveled in delightful conversation, decadent meals and adventurous excursions. GOD was revealing himself to us. Friends and family continued to communicate encouraging messages our way. The timing of one friend Amy's text was pivotal for our souls and her words so inspirational I must share them. The text was sent as Stephanie and I were wading in the waters of one of the most captivating locations on earth. I should have sensed pure joy and peace considering where we were and how personal and loving GOD was to us. My human weakness was popping up again. I hugged Stephanie and spoke something out of anxiety. *"What if God let us make this trip so that you would have some good last memories with me?"* Stephanie refused this notion, but we cried holding each other in the ocean. I knew for at least a moment this thought had also crossed her mind. We both felt drained by this emotional moment. We made our way to the beach chairs. Stephanie pulled out her phone and read the new message from Amy.

"Friend I have been praying for you every single day. You have not left my mind or heart for days. I am beyond thrilled to see you guys on this cruise. I will stand in the gap and watch God move on your behalf. I saw Shawn standing at a table. His hands were flat on the table and it looked like he was arguing a case in a courtroom like an attorney. He had that look on his face, that I know and love. You know, that side grin, like I have an ace in my pocket and you have no idea what is about to hit you kind of look. An assurance and absolute. I saw him looking at Satan right in the eye with boldness, confidence and assurance that "it is not my time" and "you will not win". There is a resolve being built inside him that is unmovable and unshakable. He (God) is so pleased, and we already know who wins!"

What imagery from her time of intercession. I accept this. Yes, Yes, Yes! The timing was perfect this message yanked us out of our funk and we returned to a place of faith.

I spent time poring over the Psalms. They capture true emotions before GOD including anguish, discouragement, hope, fear and every other emotion we still experience today. Psalms 71 and Psalms 91 were to become dear to my heart.

Treasure from
the Darkness

*Do not only see the giants, see that they
are but a speck of dust before God.*

Stephanie has beautifully captured some love from GOD we experienced on the cruise here are her words:

Bahamas Trip (June 2017)

My hand pressed my beach hat tightly as the Bahamian driver whipped us around the island as we sat on top of a roofless bus. Our last island excursion from our cruise trip. We visited two islands before this one in the previous two days. The first one, Grand Turk, our first experience laying eyes on paradise. There we took a Segway tour and enjoyed the beach.

The second excursion on Half Moon Cay, we learned about Healing Bushes from the island and read a sign in the middle of the tour that read *Strong Back*. We had no idea it was a "healing bushes and trees walking tour." It was advertised as a Nature Walk.

At that point, we knew GOD wanted us on that Healing Bush Tour. We were mesmerized by the bushes that are in our medicines. We saw trees that they call the *Tree Of Life*. The tour guide told us that the Bahama National Tree is the *Tree Of Life* and that the country is a Christian nation. We had no idea. Hot tears accompanied us while the Bahamian tour guide explained these precious truths. Here we are at the beginning of our healing journey and we end up on an island talking about Healing Medicine. Not to mention, that Shawn purchased a *Tree Of Life* journal before we boarded our cruise weeks before.

Shawn made an observation that the only printed sign on the entire tour was the sign that read *Strong Back*. It was a particular tree. We saw it as a sign that

Shawn's back will remain strong. That his bones will remain strong and heal.

My hand steadily on my hat now taking in the sights on Freeport Island. We were making our way to a private beach designed for tourists like ourselves. At this point, my heart was growing accustomed to meltdowns of deep sobbing. I did it at any given moment on the ship: outside on our deck, inside our stateroom, etc.

I lost my Dad over a month ago, Josiah was in the Middle East, and we were processing Shawn's diagnosis. It was the gigantic elephant sitting in the room everywhere we went. We took refuge in prayer, books we had along to read, writing emails to friends constantly, and staying busy on the cruise.

I wanted someone… anyone… to pray for Shawn. This Freeport Island had a church it seemed on every block as we rushed by on the bus. I wished with all my heart that I could take Shawn into one of those churches and have the Bahamian people lay hands on him and pray. But, that was a dream, my imagination, and I was desperate. It wasn't that kind of trip. We were heading to a beach for the afternoon.

Finally arrived at the beach. We were guided to beach chairs and umbrellas to shade us for comfort. Before we decided to relax, I suggested to Shawn that we look at souvenirs in those sheds set up at the gate entrance into this private beach. Our group was busy swimming in the ocean and catching the sunshine. I thought this would be a good time to beat the madness of crowds trying to buy last-minute souvenirs before we head back to the ship and make our journey home. This was our last opportunity to shop for souvenirs for our family.

We made our way to the front area where the shops were set up in like backyard sheds. The sheds were set up in a line. We were being invited to see the product. We didn't see anything we really liked yet. There was one more shed shop, the last one in the row.

The Bahamian lady came out and greeted us. I was immediately drawn to her. She wanted us there and I did not feel sales pressure from her. She gave us space to browse product. My hands started to pick things up I liked and continued to hold while looking. The Grandmotherly lady saw that I liked her product. Again, I felt something about her. I felt a kindred spirit with her.

Our conversations turned into who we were buying for in our family. That was an open door to share about our families, our nations, etc. We became instant friends with her. We were far away from home and here this woman could have easily been our loving Grandmother. Suddenly, our new friend told us the world needs GOD's love and the Holy Spirit. She began to share her Faith and that shed was pulsating the Holy Spirit and it oozed with an intoxication.

I began to cry and told her everything! Our new friend became our prayer warrior. She sat Shawn down on a chair in her shed and opened Heaven with her prayers. This woman knew GOD and He knew her! She was well seasoned in prayer and she

> moved mountains. It was incredible! You couldn't
> help but be moved to tears by her words in prayer.
> After prayer, our Bahamian friend told Shawn about
> a tea to drink that comes from their islands. Shawn
> has been drinking that tea ever since that moment
> with her. She made us promise to come back one day
> to the Bahamas and let her know that Shawn is still
> here! I did not need a church to take Shawn into on
> that island. I needed a shed.

The last day of the cruise was upon us, the ship maneuvered into Baltimore for deportation. We gazed at the city realizing this will soon be a familiar place. We uttered a prayer for our Doctor and the Johns Hopkins hospital. After gathering our luggage, we loaded the Jeep to travel home.

I received a text from a work friend Leslie. She and her daughter participated in a cancer walk while we were cruising and made a donation in my honor. She forwarded a photograph of her daughter cradling a paper lantern adorned with my name. Waterworks again, I sure was crying a lot. Is my heart being sensitized or is this a side effect of the hormone shot I wondered?

Our home is approximately an hour north of Baltimore, so the drive home was painless. We entered through our garage thrilled to see our pets. Stephanie was first inside as I contended with the heavier luggage. I entered as Stephanie exclaimed, *"Oh my goodness your family cleaned our house from top to bottom while we were away."* The blessings continued; we peered out our kitchen sliding glass door towards our deck that needed repairs. It was completely refurbished and re-stained. This was a sizable undertaking and something I had put off, aware of money needed to pay medical bills. We were overwhelmed by this tangible expression of love my family had given us. My parents went the extra mile to even buy us a new vacuum cleaner, apparently, ours was on its last leg. We called my parents to wholeheartedly thank them and set up a time to share the amazing stories from our cruise.

Treasure from
the Darkness

God's love is infinite. His love spans the entirety of his creation. His love touches the far reaches of his vast universe as well as the quiet corners of every human heart.

Emmanuel

The morning arrived that we would be introduced to Dr. Emmanuel, our oncologist at Hopkins. All I can say is wow; this was night and day compared to our local oncology visit. Despite the devastating diagnosis, he imparted hope. He conveyed the many breakthroughs being developed. The doctor explained the unusual nature of confronting advanced prostate cancer as a young man. He confirmed I belonged in a research facility like Hopkins. He predicted there is a high probability of a genetic mutation as part of the equation.

We summarized our nightmare visit with the local oncologist, the words spoken, and prognosis given. Dr. Emmanuel spoke in dissent, *"It is foolish for any doctor to predict someone's response to treatment and put a timeline on their life not even knowing how they may respond to treatment. Soon you will be firing the local oncologists; you are in good hands at Hopkins we will keep working until we find the right treatment for you."*

One of the prayers I laid before GOD in the proceeding days was how I longed for clear direction, not choices in my treatment plan. I did not want to choose an incorrect path of care. Dr. Emmanuel was an answer to this prayer. He counseled, *"Shawn, there are over sixty clinical trials going on for prostate cancer here at Hopkins. After reviewing all your information, I believe this one to be your best option. In fact, if it was my father facing what you have been diagnosed with I would suggest it for him as well."*

A powerful recommendation and answer to prayer, no choices to struggle between, instead I was given a clear path. The proposed protocol would include the standard of care which included hormone deprivation, Docetaxel chemotherapy adding in a new experimental drug known as ODM-201. Moving forward hinged on the pharmaceutical company accepting me into the trial. I side barred with the doctor about diet, *"Absolutely diet matters!"* He suggested I remove all processed meats and dairy from my diet.

I asserted I was already doing that and more. I also voiced to Dr. Emmanuel I had faith and was trusting GOD. I shared with him, *"Your name gave me a great deal of comfort when I really needed it. I even thanked God that your parents named you Emmanuel."*

He smiled and chuckled, *"I will have to tell them that and I am glad you know what that name means."*

Stephanie and I drove home expectant. Soon I would be receiving scans for submission to the drug company. Our hope was acceptance into the trial. This trial carried a prerequisite that participants could not have had radiation or Chemotherapy pre-enrollment. This meant additional treatment could not begin until the trial arrived at their decision. Delaying treatment made me nervous, but Dr. Emmanuel asserted there was a recent study suggesting the optimal time to start Chemotherapy for advanced prostate cancer was ten to twelve weeks after starting hormone deprivation. This delay would align my treatment perfectly in that window.

I dedicated some time to updating my journal and thanking GOD. I prayed not only for healing but that my relationship with him would grow deeper. As I considered my own relationship with

GOD I realized an error in my thinking. I surely saw him as my LORD, but also mostly authoritarian and not warm as I would imagine the best father would be. I recognized the problem was not GOD, but my perspective and openness to him. I pondered, what joy to perceive myself truly as a son or treasured child and not merely as one speck of dust floating through time. A peace came over me realizing GOD and I were going to grow closer through this journey, no matter the outcome and that "even if", I was loved.

In the days following our first visit with Dr. Emmanuel (I can't make myself use his last name because his first is so comforting) GOD continued revealing his boundless personal love.

I found myself testifying to others how great GOD is, how he has been carrying me through this journey, and how he has been displaying his love. I increased the time each day I was seeking his face, soaking in worship music, reading the word and researching nutrition.

People continued to extend us words of life and hope, declaring that GOD had a plan, and this was not going to be a spiral of declining health. One of my co-workers John took a mini vacation to New Orleans, while there he sent me a timely text. I was, in fact, kicking out whispers of fear at the very moment his message arrived. His text was a story about his visit to a cafe in New Orleans. In the cafe was a prayer request chalkboard allowing patrons to write a name and request. John decided to add my name to the board. John is very tall and a sizable guy so remaining under the radar is challenging for him. When John wandered up to write my name the owner noticed him and came around to chat. John revealed my set of circumstances with her and she was moved. Loretta gathered all her patrons together and appealed to GOD for my healing, John detailed the experience as powerful, deeply spiritual, and that his wife and sister had tears. His recount of the event moved us deeply. Not only had John thought of us, but a sister in the LORD who never met us was mobilizing her patrons and calling out to GOD for my healing.

We longed to become more familiar with this precious lady and her business. John forwarded me a photograph taken of the Prayer board. It displayed the name of her business on it; Loretta's Pralines. I began to do some searching and found YouTube videos about her and the business. Upon viewing multiple videos, it was clear Loretta loves GOD and stewards her business to impact the lives of others. One of the videos Stephanie and I were watching shared how Loretta provided relief to others during hurricane Katrina. In this video, there was a "GOD Wink" for Stephanie. The video showed many buildings and homes crushed by the hurricane. When there is significant property damage from a widespread natural disaster you often see spray painted insurance messages on properties. One property clearly visible in this video did not have insurance information scrawled across it; instead, it read, Keep smiling Steph. This warmed our hearts again; we were learning to keep our eyes open to GOD speaking to us in ways we overlooked before.

I received disability paperwork returned from the doctor, this step was taken in case I ever needed to be home for an extended time due to the upcoming treatments or disease progression. I skimmed through the doctor's comments and one word devoured my soul. A question on the form asked for the duration of the condition and the doctor wrote permanently. I could not help but weep, did this mean Dr. Emmanuel did not expect I could ever achieve remission? I expressed this to Stephanie and she comforted me.

Shortly after our chat, I heard a song for the first time. It became the next anthem for me. The song was "A Voice of Truth" by Casting Crowns. The lyrics ushered me to a place of prayer where I questioned GOD about words. I sensed GOD reveal words have immeasurably more jurisdictions than nearly anyone realizes. There are many voices speaking every day and we need to distinguish and believe the voice of truth.

Another breathtaking text arrived this time from a family friend, Bob. Bob was among those who prayed for me in the Life Center healing rooms. Bob also made a point to find me on Sundays and confidently speak life right to my face. This text shared how he has been standing on Psalms 91 for my life and that GOD would satisfy me with long life. He declared I would see not only my grandchildren but my great grandchildren! I contemplated Psalms 91, it mentions knowing GOD's name, resting in the shadow of the Almighty, his protection and shelter, and of course life. I thought about the names of GOD a bit and began thanking Yahweh Rapha one of the names of GOD meaning the LORD who heals. I also began seeking to understand what it means to abide in the dwelling place of the most high.

June 18 was Father's day and my morning started with a loving card from Stephanie and gifts sent from our son Josiah while he was overseas in the Middle East! The gifts were awesome. First, was a T-shirt that read "This is my cancer-fighting shirt" secondly, he sent us bible verse wall decals for our home. Josiah was staying updated daily from his mom's emails and discerned how significant words were becoming to us. You will be like a tree firmly planted by streams of water. *You will yield your fruit in season; your leaves will not wither; and whatever you do will prosper* (Psalms 1:3) now adorned our doorway.

It was Sunday again, so we went to church and the body at Life Center showered us with love and faith. Many spoke of their confidence beyond any doubt I would receive healing. Others whispered there are no fears you have decades of life yet to come.

"And the voice of Truth tells me a different story...." The music pierced the silence, such an amazing song to begin my day. I started to prepare my breakfast. My breakfasts now consisted of a concentration of foods that GOD allowed me to learn and understand promote healing to the body. I was so shocked how little I had understood about nutrition prior to this diagnosis. I was now becoming extremely knowledgeable. I kept hearing in my heart "healing is in the garden." The more I learned the more I accepted this as truth. Healthy eating was a developing passion I never would have guessed would be part of my life.

I thought about the impending medical bills and decided to borrow some money out of our 401k, planning to pay myself back over time. As I write this I am reflecting if I should have sought GOD on this rather then my own understanding. Perhaps I missed an opportunity to see him move in a marvelous fashion to provide these needed funds. At least now as I can see this missed opportunity and will approach financial needs from a place of prayer, asking for direction prior to making choices of my own reasoning.

Today was MRI of my spine day. This scan would be used to more closely examine the bone tumors seen on CT and bone scans. As I sat in the parking lot prior to the exam, I read scriptures and deeply pondered Psalms 91 and reread uplifting texts. I called out again to my father for help; I expressed how much I loved life, my wife and the earth he created. I put forth, *"I want to live, please spare me, heal me and glorify your name through my life."* I then rose up in faith and addressed the very cells of my body and declared healing. My mind began to contemplate again the nature of cancer. I comprehended these cells are so insignificant before my GOD. I shouted, *"Cancer cells, you are insignificant and pathetic compared to Jesus, I will be healed."*

The MRI lasted about an hour. During this hour-long test you cannot move, I found my mind wandering to my life with Stephanie. We have had a respectable life to this point. Yes, we had trials and tribulations, but we always had love and faith. GOD had been there for us in every storm of life and never let us suffer to a point of destruction. I reflected on Stephanie. She is the single greatest blessing I have ever known. She trusts GOD without question, always loves and because of her passion, so many people were carrying me in prayer. The hour went by more peaceful than scans in the past, my heart and mind were grateful, and my eyes were seeing how blessed my life is.

I requested a copy of my MRI for myself in addition to the file for Hopkins. At home, I loaded it into my computer. I could clearly see a few bones in my spine were contrasting differently than healthy vertebrae. A deep sorrow filled my heart. I began to cry. Am I going to die? Am I a mental case and delusional about the healing power of GOD? Should I just go out on disability and try to experience some good times with Stephanie and the kids? I was so disappointed with my faith.

One image and my heart and mind derailed again. I got control of myself and aligned my thoughts to continue the strategy downloaded to my mind. I would eat only healing foods and avoid any that promoted cancer growth. I would commit to my physical workouts and keep seeking GOD. Yes, I thought to myself I cannot earn my healing! But I can be a faithful steward of my body and do the things I know to do while trusting GOD.

I believe now when you search for revelation and desire to commune with GOD with all your heart, you begin to grasp him and his nature in day to day occurrences. Our niece Katelyn spent the night and when she woke up for the morning we offered her breakfast before we dropped her off at my mom's house for the day. She responded, *"No, that's ok. Grandma will make me pancakes!"*

"Did you already talk to her and know she is going to do this for you?"

"Nope… I just know she will!" Katelyn had confidence in the love, character, and personality of her grandmother and knew what to

expect without even checking ahead. Stephanie pointed out, this is how we need to see GOD and approach him, full of confidence for the help we need.

What a simple and yet deep revelation. We need to recognize and trust the character of GOD above all intellect or reasoning. "He's a good, good father ... that's who he is."

Treasure from the Darkness

Trust in God's character, not only his power.

Kal-El

I began my day at work attempting to be a diligent employee; keeping my body and mind as stress-free as possible. Some of my recent readings on health spoke about how the body cannot heal when we are in a stressed-out state or "fight or flight" mode. I understood now, how I pretty much lived in that state, continually worrying about issues related to work clients and potential life problems on the horizon. Worries have been the driving force in my life. I mulled to myself this is unhealthy. I must get a healthier perspective on trials. Life is so much more important than the situations I stress about.

I noticed a corner of a card sticking out from under my computer keyboard and pulled it out. I opened the envelope and inside I saw a Superman logo staring back at me. How could anyone know what this symbol means to me? I was moved. Inside the card were promises to keep me in prayer from two of my co-workers who were also twin sisters. They included a bible verse (Exodus 14:14): *The Lord will fight for you: you need only to be still.* Yes, GOD, I hear what you are saying I must trust you and learn how not to worry.

The Superman symbol had become curious to me and one of the ways GOD used my surroundings to remind me yet again "This is His". The reason it is so dear to my heart goes significantly beyond any idea of strength or being a fan of superheroes. It began with a conversation Stephanie and I had with our future daughter in law about how our future granddaughter would address us. She already called Becka's parents "Grandma and Grandpa" so coming up with other names to differentiate was the plan. For some reason being a pappy or papaw didn't seem like a fit.

I said, *"How about she calls me 'Super Shawn'?!"* As funny as it may sound the idea stuck and I became "Super Shawn" to our dear granddaughter.

I pondered to myself for a moment, I know a bit about Superman from childhood cartoons, comic books, and movies, but I speculated there is more. Why has this symbol been appearing at so many key moments? As I started to process this I considered the power of words again and suddenly my thoughts went to Superman's birth name Kal-El. Hmm, that sure does sound a lot like a Hebrew name to me. I thought of Gabriel and other names from the bible and knew El meant "GOD" or "of GOD". I opened Google and started typing "what does the name Kal-El mean?" Boom there it was staring me right in the face Kal-El in Hebrew means "Voice of GOD". I fell out of my chair to my knees.

This symbol would now stand for exponentially more to me. An article near the top of the search list perked my interest. It compared the story of Superman to Moses looking at the Jewish roots of Superman's creators. I found myself flowing from page to page and search to search learning about the creators and history of Superman. I hesitated; thinking Shawn you must be insane. Why would GOD speak to you using a Superhero symbol? He doesn't care about such things or reveal himself in ways like this. I settled there a moment, a bit deflated almost accepting this critical voice in my mind. However, a prompting inside me whispered: "Go to the source."

Does GOD ever use symbols and natural things to communicate and guide his people? Oh yes, he does! Story after story I saw clearly GOD not only used parables but symbols and day to day items to communicate with his people. This new understanding would empower me. I was enlightened to GOD speaking in ways I never had been before.

Oh my, it was practically lunchtime and I had scarcely completed any actual work. At least I am not stressed today I thought to myself. I was exhilarated with this newly acquired revelation. My phone rang, it was a local doctor's office. The voice on the phone stated, *"We have your PSA number and it is now 4.9, this is a dramatic drop for only 11 days."*

I said, *"Thank you, I will be in touch once I know if Hopkins is going to incorporate any local services."* I did the math this was an 80% drop. I was elated my body was responding to the hormone deprivation therapy.

I shared the news with Stephanie, she was incredibly upbeat. She promised, *"We will see this through. You will be healed!"* We shared the news with other family and friends and they were all encouraged.

Every day I researched nutrition and treatment breakthroughs related to prostate cancer. I discovered a newly released clinical study from the University of Texas. This study was examining natural ingredients that disrupted cancer. They were testing these on prostate cancer cells. Scientists analyzed 145 different natural compounds. The study determined certain nutrients were particularly effective at killing prostate cancer cells and slowing progression.

They proposed the concept of testing certain compounds used together. They moved forward to testing and captured remarkable outcomes. The end results unveiled three compounds exhibited synergistic effects on prostate cancer tumors. These compounds used together modulated the cells and starved them of an amino acid needed for growth. An additional promising detail was these items were food based and had no toxicity. The key items were ursolic acid found in rosemary and apple peels; curcumin found in turmeric and resveratrol found in grapes and berries. I was astonished by this research and concluded I would incorporate these compounds as supplements and foods in my diet every day.

What a remarkable day. I traveled home and shared everything with Stephanie. Our heart to heart conversations continued leading us closer and closer to each other and to our father.

June 22-30, 2017

These days of waiting between visits, scans and treatments reminded me of staring at water waiting for it to boil. I recognized GOD had the perfect path prearranged for me, but I needed to continually shake off leaning on my own understanding.

It is frequently stated you will know who your friends are when times are tough. I was stunned that so many people cared about my wife and me. There were no signs of slowing in our friends' efforts to send encouragement. I was astonished by the profession of their faith in the face of terminal cancer.

During my life, I would pray for others who had serious conditions, but I had never asked GOD what his heart was specifically for a person, or if I was to share any specific encouragements. I prayed *"If … wait I mean when I come through this please help me to be such a comforter and warrior for others."*

Sunday rolled around again, and we were off to church. At this point, there was no place I would rather be. Our church has been blessed with an abundance of faith and amazing times of worship. Today I could not focus on praising GOD during worship. My thoughts kept returning to my own need. I wondered if GOD was disappointed in me. Was I so self-centered that I could not worship GOD, the very source of the miracle I needed so badly?

The message of the day covered how people struggle to move out of comfort. One line that stood out was "Nine out of ten people wouldn't make a significant change even if their lives depended on it!"

I thought, how can that be? I will do everything and anything I can to live and beat this diagnosis. After the service, Stephanie and I wandered up front for additional prayer. Anne one of our greatest allies came over to join those already praying for us. She softly whispered, *"Shawn if someone is going to beat the diagnosis you are facing, it is you. You are waring at this from every side, medical, mental, nutrition and spiritual. You are that one in ten. Actually, you are the one in nine hundred."* She proceeded to pray for my mind knowing that overthinking was clearly my weakest link. Anne asked GOD to help me be sharp when I needed to be on the nutrition and research but dumb when it came to overthink about the things I shouldn't.

"Yes, GOD help me to not play the movies in my mind featuring the darkest outcomes."

Keeping the mind healthy is one of the hardest battles for a cancer patient. This roller coaster often had me up and down and feeling completely out of control.

Occasionally no words are necessary to convey a message. I saw a friend from my teen years Jesse, whom I have not stayed as close with as I would like over the years but have a deep respect for. He noticed me at church as his family was visiting from out of town. He wrapped his arms around me with a deep hug and I literally encountered the love of GOD. "And the greatest of these is Love." I thought to myself.

We left the church and ventured on another peaceful nature walk. We found a nice place to sit and eat a healthy lunch. We discussed the encouragement of the day and professed our faith that GOD was seeing us through. Evening came, and we retired to bed falling asleep quite peacefully.

Little did I expect to wake up with anxiety, yet the middle of my night proved to be a battle. I woke to thoughts screaming I was not worthy of being healed. Thoughts reminded me of the sins of my entire lifetime. My heart raced as if I was truly in a fight. As each thought came to the forefront of my mind I laid it before the LORD confessing and admitting my need for a savior. *"Please take these thoughts from me God."*

"These sins while great, are covered by your blood and mercy."

I was sweating and traumatized by the weight of my sins over the years being fired at me like a machine gun. Suddenly I began to sense peaceful thoughts. *"You have never been worthy in yourself, neither has any person that has ever lived. Your righteousness is as filthy rags. It is only by my blood and righteousness."*

Yes! Yes! I am covered and forgiven, and I am as Jesus to the father's eyes. He loves me far beyond what I love my own earthly children. *"Condemnation, fear, and whispers of the night …you must leave me! You must submit to the truth and blood of Jesus! I am a child of God!"* Deep peaceful sleep returned.

Monday came, and I found myself at work again. I shut my door and decided in my heart I needed to take a break to hear GOD. I must slow my mind down and hear his voice to me, for me. I asked the Holy Spirit to be with me. I told my mind to be still and stop thinking so much. I examined my heart and I thanked GOD for who he is and for his grace to all mankind. I then sat quietly. My own thoughts would pop up and I focused to silence them. I was waiting on the voice that is not my own. Finally, I was still, and two items came to my mind. *"Long will be your life, for I have said so!"* … Wow, what words could I have wanted to hear more? Then I heard, *"You are a Tenderhearted Cancer Crusader."*

I prayed, *"Lord please let these be your words and not self-thoughts regurgitated from my own mind."* I felt a peace that these words were his alone.

Even though we were surrounded by an amazing network of praying people already. I longed for as many sources of prayer support as possible. This desire led me to reach out to the CBN /700 club prayer forum. One member prayed for me in a mighty way. He had lived through his own daughter given a negative cancer diagnosis but ultimately receiving healing. His words moved my heart and boosted my courage.

Praying for You Shawn and hope the following will encourage You... *"Don't be intimidated in any way by your enemies..." (Philippians 1:28, NLT) With God on your side, there is no reason to be intimidated by your enemies... You don't have to be intimidated by cancer... It's no match for your God... Sickness cannot keep you from your destiny... God has you in the palm of His hand... Nothing can snatch you away... If it's not your time to go, you're not going to go... Don't be intimidated by the Dr's report about you... There is an anointing on your life that seals you, protects you, enables you and empowers you... God has infused you with strength... The Scripture says that you can do all things through Christ. Today, go out with confidence... Go out with boldness knowing that if God is for you, it doesn't even matter who is against you! No foe can stand against the power of Almighty God... You are empowered and equipped for victory, so don't be intimidated! Father thank You for empowering Shawn to live in victory even with a diagnosis of cancer... calm his fears and anxieties we ask, we trust that no matter what comes Shawn's way, he is safe in the palm of Your hand... Shawn won't be intimidated by anything in Jesus' name Amen."*

I began to acknowledge a truth, those who have been there themselves carry a special anointing or weight when they share or minister to a similar situation.

GOD was transforming my heart and I desired to express this with actions. Over the last week or two, I had seen a homeless man standing with a sign near an intersection I turn at daily. This time I decided I must not only pray as I pass him. I need to pull over to offer a bit more than spare change and listen to his story. I felt nervous but pulled over and gave "Joe" some cash. I inquired about his story and he was very willing to share. A fire had caused him to lose his place. He was now unable to get along with his daughter's abusive husband, so he could not live with them. I shared a bit about my journey and how my hope was in Jesus as doctors had not given me hope. He told me he also believes in Jesus and was open to my prayers for his situation. After our prayer, I told him to trust GOD and look for opportunities to come his way soon. I saw Joe only a few more times. Soon, he was no longer there, and I believed GOD provided an opportunity for him.

I shared the recent updates on my journey with a co-worker and he said to me, *"God appears to be at work in your life."* He then shared a miracle his family had experienced. Oh, the value of testimonies. Hearing stories of GOD healing and saving lives triggers the heart to say, "Yes GOD is able!"

Treasure from
the Darkness

No one is worthy, except one, Jesus.

Healing is in the Garden

One of our newest passions was learning to eat healthily. My whole family has jumped on board at different levels. My parents spent half the day with Stephanie and me on a trip to an all-natural healthy grocery store. It is so very exciting to see niche stores that have organic heirloom vegetables, fruits and grains. I felt like we were back in time. Everyone there was happy, friendly and healthy. Every time I learned about a store or source of healthy foods, I would check it out. It became increasingly clear to me that Americans do not eat well. I know this is obvious with a fast food joint every block, but I mean beyond that. So many processed foods, GMO foods, and so little healthy fruits and vegetables. Our meats are extremely different than those of just a few generations ago. Today you pay a premium for healthy items as the latest industrial farming procedures are driven by efficiency. I will step off this topic for now, but I could write a whole other book on nutrition and food in America.

It was Sunday afternoon and a longtime friend Tammy called. She invited us over to swim and socialize but there was more behind the invite. Tammy advised us she had another friend also coming over, who had just received a cancer diagnosis. Tammy's friend needed encouragement and council. Tammy sensed I had the grace to talk with her. Stephanie and I agreed to come over. Inside I was conflicted. One part of me was like yes; I will speak faith and life and share all I have learned. The other part of me shouted, you still have cancer you are going to share advice but with what authority. Fear is a horrible enemy. It twists, pokes and pulls at the deepest most sensitive areas of a soul. I'm beginning to believe that fear's assignment is to keep us on the bench. To prevent us from using the strength and glory we sense is inside of us through Christ. I recalled the verse in Timothy GOD has not given us a spirit of fear, but of power, Love and a sound mind. I decided even if, I will stand in faith and speak boldly of his love and healing power. I will share all I am learning about nutrition and its ability to heal the body. My words that night lifted her spirits and boosted her courage.

Stephanie and I have always enjoyed strolls in nature, escaping to chat about life, dreams, joys, and fears. Studies clearly indicated those more physically active have superior cancer outcomes. I decided I needed to leave no stone unturned. We increased our commitment to keeping me moving. At minimum three times a week, we would venture somewhere to take long brisk walks. These times were not only healthy for our bodies but our souls.

Have you ever thought you knew everything about your spouse and loved them as much as you possibly could? I felt that about Stephanie. I considered our marriage a treasure and our understanding of each other's' hearts a rare precious gift. Somehow my love was expanding to new and deeper levels. I knew she had strength, but I never witnessed it on the level I was now. A journey like we were on has the potential to damage relationships due to pain, fear and the challenges associated with it. Every day she was there for me. Praying, encouraging, and giving me strength. Stephanie is my greatest blessing in life. Occasionally I struggled with two thoughts simply because of my great love for her. Could and would I have been the strength for her that she is to me if roles were reversed? The second was how the thought of leaving her broke my heart. I would not want her to suffer or feel alone for even a moment. Amazing love stories entice people to read or watch movies, here I am living one.

July 4, 2017

If GOD loves me as much as my family, he is beside me every step of this trial I thought to myself as my mother showed up again with another meal. Sure enough, my sister and her kids dropped by again as well. They wanted to spend some time together so we all watched a good family movie and enjoyed the evening. Going through a serious health diagnosis like cancer is frightening but imagine the horror it must be to do it alone and without faith. That must be a dark and lonely road.

July 5, 2017

I went to the YMCA tonight with Stephanie, fitness was now part of my journey. While no couch potato I needed to kick things up a notch. I again experienced the power of words and support. Stephanie teaches a fitness class a couple of times a week at the local Y. When I entered her class, I was immediately greeted with smiles, kind words, and encouragement from members who are close to Stephanie and know the situation. I could not help but feel loved and amazed. I would hear regular stories about Stephanie's classes, but now I was meeting these friends she held dear and experiencing the atmosphere this Y has created that she would often brag about.

Unfortunately, as easily as it was to be encouraged by words they can also be a setback. I heard a story of a member at the Y who lost their husband to cancer. Even though I was on a different path it hit me deep. "Could I someday be just a story talked about? Oh, he was a fighter. He gave it his all etc…"

I shared my thought with Stephanie as we lay in bed. My words hurt her. Stephanie had been encouraged by the evening and here I was pondering death again. I found myself trying to think my way out of this situation and realized again I could not. I then heard words from a worship song in my mind…" Your Love never fails, it never gives up, it never runs out on me. "I drifted to sleep singing this in my mind.

July 6, 2017

Today was a healthier day. I woke up refreshed and thankful to be alive. Stephanie sent an email to our praying friends. I soon started receiving encouraging texts and messages uplifting my spirit. I dedicated some time to explore GOD's word, searching for what it looks like to live by faith. As I was studying I realized that relying on my own reasoning and understanding was not new for me. It was, in fact, the way I approached life in general. How often did I seek GOD for his wisdom or guidance first rather than trusting my own wisdom? I decided I would invest my heart more into what GOD was requesting of me. In my readings, I saw I was not the only one who wrestled with fear. It is a struggle almost everyone in the Bible faces in their journey with GOD.

Could others who have hiked Cancer Mountain have wisdom for me? I searched for stories of cancer survivors who were victorious and had some advice to share. I fell upon a PDF a Christian man wrote providing tips for the journey. I devoured it fervently searching for tools for my life. A few bullet points jumped out at me. They were; resting the mind and body, trusting GOD's plan, and to keep making plans for the future. These caught my eye because I needed them for my journey. I immediately decided I would not stop making future plans. Better yet, I would make plans to benefit others.

July 7, 2017

I pondered, what undertaking could I begin that amounts to planning for the future and giving of myself? A cancer walk I reasoned. I could raise funds for research against the disease I am diagnosed with. I searched online for prostate cancer walks. Prostate Zero an established non-profit had an event scheduled in Harrisburg in a few months. I decided I would create a team, perhaps some family and friends would join me raising money for the cause. As I established my team on their website I advanced to a line requesting a team name. I pondered it for a moment and settled on Team Super Shawn.

In the evening I received a phone call. On the other side of this call was the Mid Atlantic Director of Prostate Zero. She wanted to welcome my team to the walk but called me personally to find out a bit more of my story. She mentioned my team name jumped out at her because of her name. When she shared her name with me I was astounded. Her name is Shawn Supers. We both laughed and reveled a bit in this serendipitous naming. We then continued discussing the upcoming walk and team captain details. In my heart, I perceived this was a divine connection that someday may lead to opportunities to share and bring hope to others. Suddenly a negative thought whispered, "What are you thinking? What do you have to share?" "You might not even be alive in September. "I constrained the negative voice and resolved to hold onto the good thought as a revelation about the future.

July 9, 2017

When I consider Life Center and why it is such a precious community to worship with, l am reminded of a video I once caught on Facebook. The lady sharing taught how the environments we create transform surroundings and even attracts things. In her presentation, she uses the example of an overturned boat resting near a pond on their property. Prior to the boat being placed and flipped upside down in the grass. The environment was simply grass. However, once the boat settled there upside down for a week or two the environment changed. Flipping it right side up could now cause you to squirm a bit. Knowing there would be centipedes, snakes, slugs, and toads ready to race every direction the moment you move the boat. She questioned why are they there? No one transplanted them to this location. They drew near due to "the environment". We also create environments in our lives. Do our churches, homes and other environments welcome GOD and his presence? At Life Center, the answer is definitely yes!

Today's message was on trusting the promise even when we do not understand the process. Inside I conceded, "Yes LORD, help me to trust you despite my ability to see how the details all play out". "I believe you will heal me I just don't fully know how the details play out."

After the service, I received more prayers and encouraging words of faith. GOD will have victory in your life, there will be a book and you will teach others. There is no doubt GOD will heal you and you will be victorious! What an environment of faith, no wonder GOD moves in this place. He is welcomed here twenty-four hours a day.

July 10, 2017

I spent time in devotions and read John 16:33. I kept reciting to myself repeatedly *"But he has overcome the world."* I decreed to focus on the kingdom and not only my struggles.

We received an e-mail from a seasoned cancer prayer warrior friend Deborah. She asked us if we were speaking declarations over my body. She also provided us a link to a book containing powerful healing declarations based on scriptures. This was not something I was doing. I reviewed the declarations and read the associated theology. I started to speak the promises and words of life, at first softly but with increasing boldness. I could not have imagined the response I would feel. My faith began to rise as I declared GOD's promises over my life. This was going to be something I would do every day.

Stephanie and I took another walk. I received a call confirming my first screening date for the clinical trial was on July 25. This would include full body scans again. Deep down I desired to see no disease progression on a clinical report, even more, I longed to see the cancer had diminished or was completely eradicated.

Friends and family all week shared with Stephanie and me, stories of people who had advanced disease yet had fantastic outcomes, overcoming the odds. These stories greatly encouraged our faith and we would say, "Do it again LORD!"

During our nature hikes, I began to perceive beauty I overlooked before. The best way to describe how I was now seeing does not come from mere words. It is more successfully illustrated by viewing a video. The video I'm referencing is almost any video of a color-blind person wearing glasses allowing them to visualize color for the first time.

Most of us appreciate the gift of color, but we are not enthralled to the depth and magnitude as someone experiencing it for the first time. Every detail was becoming more vibrant and beautiful, how awe-inspiring the universe GOD created is. Why was I constantly rushing through life? Why was I habitually discontent? Why did I over and over feel something was absent from my life? Thank you GOD, for eyes that are beginning to see.

July 18, 2017

Some days are roller coaster days. I received several generous donations towards my prostate cancer team's fundraising effort. Additionally, I received an e-mail from a nonprofit cancer organization a co-worker introduced me to. The email indicated they were awarding me a $2,500 grant to assist with my medical expenses. I was extremely blessed and thankful. I sensed circumstances were continuing to fall into place, my needs were being met and I was being chauffeured through this trial. Suddenly I received a phone call that pulverized my joy. I had completed a DNA test to determine if any mutations were contributing to the cancer diagnosis. The results were completed; I carried a defective BRCA 2 gene. This defect was tied to many types of cancers and increased risks. While cancer is frightening enough the hardest part to digest was the 50% chance this gene was passed down to my children. A chance also existed it originated from my mother and could exist in my brother and sister and their children. I was overwhelmed with tears, I had to leave work. I pleaded to GOD, *"Lord please spare my family."* I bounced back to a place of faith again as I prayed. I returned to the declarations, declaring words of hope and healing. I realized this gene had been within me since birth, GOD is not surprised by any of the events unfolding.

July 20, 2017

I yearned to remain near to GOD. I lingered in long sessions of worship and prayer. I still experienced discouragement within my heart. Why was I tossed back and forth? Why could I not keep my faith strong nonstop? Was this BRCA 2 revelation going to crush my hope? I read a devotional and sensed GOD imparting a gracious revelation of his love and gentleness, despite my internal struggles. The devotion focused on the first half of Psalms 142:3 when my spirit was overwhelmed within me, then you knew my path. The writer proceeded to discuss David being in despair while writing certain Psalms and despite his pain, GOD was perfectly near him. David while composing this Psalm realized even though his spirit was overwhelmed GOD was in control.

GOD is not taken by surprise with my struggles and discouragement. He is with me even now. He created me, knows my nature and thought processes. I longed to die to my flesh and walk in faith but allowed myself grace to work through my genuine sorrow. GOD is gracious, and he knows my path.

I researched BRCA 2 and located a myriad of bad news tied to this genetic dysfunction. I sensed a nudge in my heart to go a different route. "Look up how it responds to foods and therapies. "I returned to research and my heart leaped. I found a study that indicated BRCA 2 forms of cancer were three times more responsive to flavonoid treatments then wild forms of cancer. GOD had already been leading me to nutrition, He knows my path!

Treasure from
the Darkness

*Fear wants to immobilize you. As soon as you step out
in faith you will see he has overcome the world.*

Puzzle Pieces

July 21, 2017

My morning reading was (Romans 4:20-21): *Yet he did not waver through unbelief regarding the promise of God but was strengthened in his faith and gave glory to God, 21 being fully persuaded that God had the power to do what he had promised.* I prayed, *"Yes God may my faith grow."*

I decided to visit the healing room at Life Center again. I needed a fresh round of prayers to strengthen and seal my growing faith, boosted by the recent revelations. What a precious experience the healing room is. Many seasoned faith-filled prayer warriors joining with you to lay your burden before the lord. A few impressions occurred within people's hearts and they expressed them.

"GOD is being glorified through you and others are being moved towards Christ through your journey."

"GOD promises to you will be fulfilled and you will see your grandchildren."

"You will be used for a glorious purpose and bring amazement to the medical community."

"You will give hope to others."

"You must stay close to GOD, do not give in to the fear of bad reports, and believe his report".

"Your family and children will not be shackled with the curse."

"He is already healing you."

"You are being changed and his glory and presence are resting on you."

"You are growing in GOD and his purposes."

"Psalms 91 is for you."

Wow, my hope was fully recharged. Prayer teams need to be a component of our healthcare system. Prayer and spiritual support for patients is vital.

July 22, 2017

So frequently our lives consist of days of going through the motions. We keep up our normal patterns and simply view them as days to get through until the weekend or our next big event. Is this how we are meant to live? Are we missing something? Is it our routines that need to be changed or our hearts or both? It must be both I reasoned to myself. It is impossible for everyone to live on permanent vacation, there are mundane tasks that require attention, but we cannot devote so much of our lives to the mundane that we have no time remaining for the meaningful.

Our hearts should never sleepwalk through life. Wake up spirit, view each day differently, eyes wide open, heart fully awake. Teach me LORD, to live differently, more meaningfully. I longed not for the pursuit of happiness but the pursuit of meaning. I was reminded of an old book I had read over twenty years ago. "Practicing the presence of GOD". I decided to read it again. My answer was living in an ongoing conversation with GOD throughout the entire day.

Yes, I desired to live and honor GOD but any special purpose for my life? Such thoughts had become only faded dreams from my youth. I had accepted my destiny was to live a simple life of limited purpose. Could GOD be waking me up for a second act in life?

July 22, 2017

Stephanie and I embarked on another of our long walks and shared the deepest parts of our hearts with one another. We spoke words of life and repeated the promises GOD had given us. After our walk, we visited a book store and drank some coffee and read. As we relaxed I saw a much older couple doing the same thing. I whispered to Stephanie, *"I want that to be us someday so bad."*

In a very assuring tone, Stephanie whispered back, *"It will be!"*

July 23, 2017

I was in my secret place, my holy of holies, the shower in my bathroom. I was spending a lot of time in the shower praying and worshiping. Today was a Sunday so I looked forward to the worship and community at Life Center. When worship ended, and people returned to their seats I sat down and found a painted rock in a little bag left for me. The stone had the word believe painted in bright colors. Another beautiful message of hope, hand delivered.

After the service people spoke with me. Unfortunately, not everyone was encouraging. One of the people who talked with me was a medical professional and they decided to reiterate the magnitude of the disease state I was in and the expected outcome. I thought to myself why even talk to me about this I know what the doctors, science, and internet say.

As soon as this conversation ended Stephanie showered me with words of life …" but that's not you!"

A storm rolled through our area as evening came. Stephanie and I popped open camping chairs in the garage and with the door open watched a storm in its power and splendor. I thought about how much of life I had taken for granted. I was not alone in this storm many were with me.

July 24, 2017

Stephanie shared some imagery I found meaningful. In my heart, I was longing for an instant miracle of complete healing. She revealed, *"Each small miracle we experience is a puzzle piece of the whole puzzle which is our miracle."* I thought about her words and decided GOD's ways are better than mine. I desire his plan, I know it will impact the most lives with his love.

Treasure from
the Darkness

*Not everyone who speaks into your life is
speaking as an ambassador from God.*

In the Valley

July 25, 2017

My brother James arrived long before sunrise for our journey to Johns Hopkins. I would be receiving many scans and labs for submission to the clinical trial. Stephanie and I decided she would remain home and go to work saving time off for chemo days when I would need her more.

My heart raced during each scan, I noticed the equipment at Hopkins was faster and more comfortable than the local machines. While in scans I would sing worship songs in my heart. I would also speak declarations in my mind over my body. Beyond the scans and labs, I had a large amount of paperwork and questionnaires to complete. It was a long day, but I felt hopeful the scans were going to show I was already healing.

My brother and I made our way to the hotel for the night. I was scheduled to return the next day to meet with the doctor to review scans and discuss any changes on the submissions to the drug company. Shortly after we settled in the hotel I received an email from my patient portal indicating my scans had uploaded. As I was on the phone with Stephanie I brought up the information. Little did I know I was about to have the worst night of my life.

I read the scan information and began to panic. A surge of dread and physical pain overwhelmed me. It was like I had been hit by a truck. The scans did not present the healing I expected to see. The reports indicated lesions that were never mentioned before. Four additional spine vertebrae were noted as having lesions, a rib, my left scapula, and my right hip bone. How could this be? I began having a panic attack. Am I going to lose this battle and die? I could not even maintain a conversation with my beloved wife. I curled up in bed and entertained fearful thoughts of pain, suffering, death and the loss my family would experience.

I tossed and turned all night, my mind bouncing between terror and desperate prayers. Stephanie alerted our prayer team, friends and family. Many texts of prayers and scriptures came through the night. I was loved, but it looked like cancer was going to have its way.

July 26, 2017

I forced myself to rise after a sleepless night. My battered mind told me I was not to quit my nutrition protocol. I was so dedicated I lugged a blender and cooler to the hotel just so I could remain diligent while traveling.

I plopped down in the waiting room, a prisoner shackled by fear. Every second of the clock seemed an hour. I lumbered to the bathroom and noticed the toilet seat cover dispenser read "rest assured". Obviously, their brand or tagline yet somehow the words jarred my thoughts. Perhaps a "GOD Wink" to be positive?

Finally, I was escorted to review scans with the medical team. To my bewilderment, the nurse practitioner did not immediately express any angst over the scans, so I spoke up. I questioned the new lesions and the disease progressing. Her interpretation would have spared me a night of torment. She explained Hopkins has advanced equipment and these are not new lesions, they were already there. Several were centimeter size. This provided me a bit of comfort but as I considered the way my body was feeling I recognized discomfort in the mentioned locations.

Arriving home, Stephanie and I walked and processed the experiences and struggles of the previous two days. We stopped at a local store and as we entered a lady was exiting. She was wearing a T-shirt adorned with the phrase "Never ever give up!" Stephanie and I smiled and agreed we would never give up.

It is difficult to keep your faith fervent while contrary information is thrust in your face. I must find the key to keep my eyes on Jesus. I prayed again while taking a hot shower, I sensed GOD loves me, is righteous, and many believers are standing with me. I will be healed and share my testimony. Once again *"THIS"* popped in my mind. This is his. After the shower, I conveyed to Stephanie, *"There are many trails and paths in life, but we are on the one he has marked for us."*

July 27, 2017

Back to work. I found myself engaging in heartfelt conversations with co-workers concerning life and GOD. Stephanie and I both around this time started to receive emails and communications from others struggling with cancer journeys. I wondered why they are reaching out to us. We are enduring and toiling on our path. Yet somehow others were receiving encouragement from us as if we were victors. I am convinced they perceived the faith, hope, and love that were at work in our lives. They saw Jesus.

July 28, 2017

Stephanie and I made a point to head over to her grandmother's house. During this visit, a very sweet moment occurred. My wife's aunt has a friend named Carl who was also visiting. Carl participates in many of our family events. Carl is a sweet yet often timid person. He recently took a trip to Europe and visited a Catholic pilgrimage site renowned for healing holy water. Carl captured a bottle of this water and carries it everywhere. He considers it precious and something he needs to have with him. Carl spoke with me about the water and inquired if I wanted some. I am not Catholic but knew we both loved Jesus. I also saw Carl's precious heart. I secured a few drops and anointed my head and we prayed for my healing. Carl and I both wept a bit. Carl then pronounced, *"I believe God is going to heal you."* I pondered this moment processing how GOD considers our hearts. I imagined there are many instances we allow our intellect or denominational upbringing to hinder an expression of GOD's love.

July 29, 2017

I awoke from a dream that energized my heart. I dreamt the pain I felt in my bones recently was in fact my bones healing. Within my dream, I visualized small voids in my bones created from cancer restored with new healthy bone cells. I was inspired to reread my latest CT and bones scans, so I did. I had been so focused on newly noted lesions I overlooked some amazing changes. My prostate had originally been described as enlarged and asymmetrical with a lump on the left posterior and now it was described as normal size and shape. Previously a number of lymph nodes had been enlarged they were now normal size. These were both clinical improvements that I was blinded to by fear and anxiety. Keep the healing flowing GOD!

Today was an annual picnic we attend with our best friends and their children. We participated in normal picnic activities enjoying each other's company. The tribe congregated around me and expressed a desire to pray and minister to me. As a token of love, they presented a jar of cash raised among themselves, even the working teens contributed. The cash was to aid me in paying medical expenses. This priceless vessel was adorned with lettering spelling out "*THIS*" clearly restating my vision "This is his."

Our beloved friends also presented me two additional treasures, a box of cards with scriptures each person had discerned were for my life and a painting one of the pre-teens had perfected for me. I was so touched; the atmosphere of love was very tangible to all. A few of the prayers and words spoken hit me as treasures to keep hold of. Our one friend, Vince, mentioned while praying he envisioned us walking on a beach holding hands celebrating a successful journey. Libby shared how she had never prayed for someone as much as she has me. For some reason, the words that clung to my heart the most were from our friend James who pulled me aside later to share his impression. During prayers he visualized a stone thrown in the water, ripples proceeded outward in every direction, that is your life and your journey. Your life will influence others beyond what you can imagine or know. This imagery James shared would come back to me many times.

July 30, 2017

This Sunday was going to be an uplifting day. During an early worship song, I noticed Sue a number of rows in front of us. Sue is an incredible faith warrior who has been victorious in a no hope cancer diagnosis. Quietly I was half thinking, half praying I would love it if she would pray for me. No more than a few moments after that thought I spot both Sue and Anne marching back to pray for me. They came armed with a testimony ready to share.

The text they received was from a lady fighting advanced cancer. She had received her most recent test results displaying great improvement. The healing taking place was significant enough it shocked her oncologist. After sharing this news, they began to pray for me. Sue in her very powerful and passion filled voice declared words boosting my faith. *"God is fixing you and mending you on the inside. Signs and wonders will follow your testimony. He loves you so much. Long life. Victory."* Sue returned to her seat just as the worship team started to sing a song about GOD being our victory. Sue spun around and pointed at me.

While this prayer session was taking place, Stephanie was off worshiping and dancing. A lady approached her and remarked, *"I have a word for you and your husband. Can I catch you guys after the service?"* Once the service ended this lady and her husband came over. She declared, *"I do not know what you're going through, but God wants me to tell you he will bring you through this and that you will minister hope to others."* I revealed the diagnosis we were facing; I observed some non-verbal cues that she may have been in shock she just spoke a word of life to someone contending with a terminal cancer diagnosis.

Later in the afternoon, our nurse friend Sunny sent us a video link of "sheep know their master's voice". The video showcased a crowd of onlookers behind a fence surrounding a herd of sheep. Members from this on looking group attempted to attract the sheep to come over. The sheep remained completely unfazed by their calls, whistles, and shouts. Suddenly the Shepherd voices a call. The sheep instantly recognize their master's voice and respond with bleats while scurrying to him. Oh, how dearly I long for that level of discernment when GOD speaks. I desire the ability to separate my thoughts, fears, and imaginations from the true voice of GOD. After watching this video, I prayed *"Lord, teach me to only listen to the voice of truth."*

July 31, 2017

Before leaving our bedroom Stephanie and I start our morning in prayer. I admire her never-ending love for me and fortitude to keep this a priority.

I spoke with some friends of ours on a similar journey with terminal cancer. I listened to their most recent reports. After the chat, I prayed for them wholeheartedly. I thought about how at times we speculate GOD's healing is a limited well or pool of water. If this was the truth, there would only be so much to go around for miracles. How foolish to imagine this consciously or subconsciously? GOD is limitless with more than enough for all his children. The secret must be aligning our lives with his truths and will. I spent some time considering my son Josiah and how excited I was he would soon be returning safely from serving in the Middle East.

I invested some time on the mind-body connection doing positive visualizations of my future. As I prayed and considered my future, I found myself visualizing a beautiful motion-picture in my mind. Stephanie and I were dancing as a healthy elderly couple. I was seeing this from an on-looker's perspective and distinguished out of all the couples on the floor we radiated a love that was unmatched. Joy filled my heart.

Treasure from
the Darkness

Our life makes ripples in the lives of others;
your actions or words today could impact generations.

Normal Thyroid

August 1, 2017

A new month, the month of my birth and this year I was soon turning 44. We had yard work that needed to be completed and Stephanie picked up a lot of the slack. While working I received an email that the trial PSA lab report loaded to my medical chart. The PSA number is a blood marker that indicates the activity level of prostate cancer and measures the response to therapy. I had not started chemo or the trial drug yet, but I was on a hormone deprivation treatment intended to slow growth of the cancer.

As I loaded the report my heart fluttered. I have been in such a positive mindset expecting nothing but healing but now I would be seeing a clinical report. What would it indicate? My PSA originally was 24, and then dropped once deprivation started to 4.9. This most recent report indicated 1.46! Yes! I thought this is moving in the right direction and a marvelous report. I knew the all-important number I needed was less than 0.1, it was not there but I was encouraged. GOD, please teach me to celebrate small victories and not reason that I cannot rejoice for any report except remission.

August 2-4, 2017

Our son arrived home from his deployment in the Middle East. This allowed our minds to no longer carry the additional concern of his safety. I found myself improving in the ability to kick out fearful thoughts that try to creep in throughout my days. One strategy that proved very successful was to play an old worship song over and over in my mind, "Turn your eyes upon Jesus, look full in his wondrous face."

The ownership team at my work decided they would organize a team to participate in the Zero Prostate cancer walk in September. "Team McConkey" would come on-board with "Team Super Shawn". My employer offered to pay half the registration fees for those who joined and went as far as to allow attendees to leave work a bit early the day of the event.

August 6, 2017

It was Sunday, again I felt refreshed by prayers, the worship and focusing my heart on GOD as my creator. Stephanie and I escaped to a book store to read a bit and savor some coffee. I discovered a book on "Radical Remission". This book's author studied the commonalities of survivors who beat the odds and astonished the medical community by coming through to the other side of dire cancer diagnoses. The author interviewed these survivors and analyzed their stories, ultimately categorizing and expounding upon the key common factors. I read and pondered if I was already doing these things. Amazingly enough, I was engaging in almost all the key items. I had taken ownership of my health, I transformed my diet to be organic plant-based, I was employing certain supplements to boost my immune system and battle cancer, I delved deep into my spiritual connection with GOD, and I had a strong support system.

Out of the key commonalities, the book identified I only observed three I needed to improve on or add to my journey. I needed to focus on the positive, why I desire to live vs. not wanting to die and enjoying life not fighting cancer in my mind every moment of every day. I committed to improving in these areas.

August 9, 2017

Stephanie and I were on way to Hopkins; this time for an MRI of my thyroid. The clinical trial CT scan identified a growth on my thyroid. I was nervous but hoping it would be benign and not connected to the cancer.

The tech started the MRI scan of my neck, I felt his frustration rising and increasing intensity as he scanned my neck. He proceeded to shove the scanner with greater force into my neck, eventually changing attachments and many settings on his equipment. After manhandling my throat considerably longer than expected he huffed *"I'll be right back I need to speak to the doctor."* My imagination started to entertain my reoccurring nemesis Fear. Did they discover more cancer? Beads of sweat rolled down my face as I waited for his return. The tech reappeared and stated, *"OK, you're done."*

In the waiting room, I revealed to Stephanie the difficult scan and how I discerned something was very off considering how hard he pressed, his frustration levels and the need to speak to a doctor. My memories of the night after the trial scans came rushing back. I had believed for good news and instead received scans with additional lesions. However, in the end, the doctor's advised nothing new had occurred and there indeed were clinical improvements. I counseled myself to calm down and trust GOD. Right after I thought I fully convinced myself, an image of fear flashed into my mind. The image was of a tombstone with my name on it. I prayed to GOD for help my mind and heart were under attack.

Later in the evening the MRI scans uploaded to my chart. I opened it up trembling a bit. The results caused me to cry, this time happy tears. The report indicated my thyroid was thoroughly examined and no nodule exists, in fact, written on the report was completely normal thyroid. Stephanie and I praised GOD for the good news. In hindsight the manhandling of my neck made sense. The tech was advised there was a nodule that required more detailed scans and he could not locate it! I recognized my body was healing.

August 10, 2017

Stephanie arranged a birthday party for me. She inspired all family and friends to show up wearing Superman shirts. The party was five days before my birthday as I had a tentative Hopkins trip on that actual day. I received thoughtful gifts and encouraging words.

I knew some people may consider this Superman connection flaky, but I knew GOD was speaking to me with symbols, dreams and day to day experiences. I decided to keep this close to my heart and only share with my closest friends and family.

Another remarkable event came about. During my birthday party, I received an email announcing I was accepted into the clinical trial. The drug company would commence the blind randomization on the coming Monday. I would have a 50/50 chance to receive the actual drug or a placebo. The trial is double-blind, so my doctor would not even be aware if I had the real deal. The letter also scheduled me to receive the trial drug or placebo in a few days. The appointment would be the morning after my actual birthday. This news also meant chemo treatments would begin. This conflicted within me. Yes, I desired the chemo melting away the cancer, but dreaded the horror stories I had heard of chemo.

August 12, 2017

We elected to enjoy the day with our children by embarking on a countryside train excursion. It was a pleasant distraction as I focused on the splendor of the view and my love for my family. On the route home, we decided to stop by a landmark in Reading, PA known as the Pagoda. This landmark rests majestically overlooking the city. It was a turn of the century hotel constructed in an Asian architectural style. The hotel never succeeded but the building now remains a fascinating tourist attraction. Interestingly enough an aspect derived from its location captured our attention more than the architecture.

As we paused looking out at the city below, it appeared to be far in the distance. Astonishing all of us was the sounds we could clearly distinguish. Voices and sounds traveled well enough to our vantage point we could differentiate the voices of children, laughs, whistles and even identify words. I never conceived sound traveling such distances in a discernible fashion. I paused for a moment and thought about the myriad of voices calling out to GOD daily.

Treasure from the Darkness

Your Father in heaven has individual and precious thoughts about you; open your heart and ask him.

Middle Name is Fearless

August 13, 2017

Sunday arrived again. The worship was healing to my soul. Tiffany and John were leading today, their songs and voices channel an intimacy with GOD few others can. In recent weeks, a wealth of people had taken time to pray for me at church. I nonetheless treasured every single prayer. I would be attentive for what GOD may be relaying to me through their prayers. Today had signs of being extra noteworthy. I had cherished friends Linda and Mark give me a birthday gift. It was a Superman ornament that played the Superman theme song, what genuinely grabbed me about the gift was the box. Printed on the box was the description "a symbol of hope".

An additional beloved friend also named Linda painted a work of art. It was the silhouette of a man worshiping. It featured this man encircled by what could be conveyed as a beautiful fog or GOD's glory. This man was moving forward pressing into this glory. She titled her painting "stepping into the atmosphere" and disclosed the man was me.

Stephanie and I made our way to the altar after the service. We had determined in our hearts we would continue this until I was healed. This week we did not know the couple praying for us, however, they imparted encouragement and a new notion for me to consider. The encouragement arrived when one of them spoke: *"God is very pleased with you, that you trust him for your healing."* Following up after this word one of them uttered *"I feel like I should ask you to talk with God and ask him, what can he teach you through this cancer journey that you have been unable or unwilling to learn any other way."* I recognized I needed to follow through on this. Never had I asked GOD if there was something I must learn or rework in my heart amidst this journey.

Later that evening I decided to take a shower and spend time in prayer. I turned on worship music and presented my heart to GOD again. I voiced to GOD my desire to go on living. How fully I loved life and my family. I thanked GOD for the work in my heart and miracles I was experiencing thus far. I declared he is GOD and ultimately, I desire his will. As torturous as it was to come to terms with, I even prayed, *"God if you will receive more glory from my death than my life please give me peace about it."*

I did not sense I was to accept dying. My heart was reminded of the words earlier that day suggesting I petition GOD about what I could learn from my journey. As I released my heart to listen for GOD to convey his heart to me I suddenly became aware of my life in its entirety and heard in my heart, *"You live your whole life in fear."*

My mind and heart began to showcase so many areas I had let fear rule me. I was continually worrying about the future, about all the what-ifs; I was without fail carrying emotional weight. This was a merciful revelation from GOD. I repented, asking him to forgive me for a life of not trusting, for leaning on my own strength, for placing temporary trust in knowledge and resources. I collapsed in the tub and continued to repent. I experienced a peace come over me and knew this was an element of my healing. I then proceeded to do something that may or may not be the best idea. I pleaded with

GOD, *"Please confirm to me the work I feel you have just done in my heart."* Pandora was continuing to play worship music, so I asked, *"God if this is your work in me, please let the next song confirm this moment. Let it mention or be about not living in fear."*

The next song began to play, it was a melody I never recalled hearing before. What played was the song "Lions" by Skillet. The entire song is about being bold and not being fearful, in fact, one line hit me deep. "Like our middle name is fearless". Often you hear someone say my middle name is "fill in the blank" with a word that denotes power or experience in an area. I certainly did not want to continue being a slave to fear, I desired to be bold enough to declare my middle name is fearless. I became overwhelmed with GOD's love for me. The GOD of the universe just lavished personal time with me in my shower. As I worshiped, I experienced a tremendous weight lifted from my back.

A secondary reason this song was perfect is my biological father had given me a rather unusual middle name. The name was associated with Greek mythology and a guardian of Hades. All my life I struggled with this name. Stephanie had recently shared with me she felt I was to change my middle name. One of the names we had considered for the future was "Caleb". One of the meanings we discovered for Caleb was faithful or wholehearted. Was this all raveled together? Was GOD telling me I was created to be wholehearted and fearless for him?

August 14, 2017

I awoke feeling spectacular reminiscing on my experience the evening before. My pain and the sensation of carrying a weight on my back had not returned. I devoted some time to reading and became focused on Psalms 112:7-8: *They will have no fear of bad news; their hearts are steadfast, trusting in the Lord. Their hearts are secure, they will have no fear; in the end, they will look in triumph on their foes.* Wow LORD, may I live in this type of victory.

Stephanie and I discussed what GOD was teaching us and planting in our hearts. We pondered the power of words yet again and how they impact us. Our thoughts expanded to realize they impact not only us but everyone. How often have we not chosen our words wisely or in a deliberate fashion expressing love and advancing the kingdom?

I had an epiphany, when we return to Hopkins again we will bring words of life with us. We can obviously speak life to anyone we enter conversations with but what about those we never talk to. I exclaimed to Stephanie, *"We should wear T-shirts with words of life across them to encourage others who see us in the waiting room or walking down a hallway."* We took a trip to the mall and purchased shirts for the upcoming chemo visit. Stephanie chose one that read "Victory is ours" and I one that read "Live Fearless".

August 15, 2017

Today was my birthday, I am now 44. My morning devotions could not have been more appropriate. I pondered a verse that never caught my eye before, Psalms 68:20, *"Our God is a God who saves; from the sovereign Lord comes escapes from death."* As I read the words, my mind flashed with images of every miracle story I had ever heard. Images of soldiers who lived beyond explanation and healings that defied scientific reason filled my mind. My escape from death is in the hands of GOD. I was encouraged and excited about what GOD was weaving into my heart and it was bubbling over in my conversations. I shared with several co-worker's recent updates on my journey and GOD's faithfulness. One of my co-workers invited me to chat a bit in his office. We thanked GOD together for his faithfulness and prayed for favor tomorrow as I returned to Hopkins to receive the trial drug. I testified of my recent experiences and the verses GOD had been leading me to. We both set about the remainder of our day with heightened faith.

After work, we loaded the car and headed to Baltimore. Our plan was to hang around and embrace the evening prior to my morning appointment at Johns Hopkins. Our hearts were overflowing with expectation and our conversations about the handiwork of GOD. We spoke life and anticipation of the finalized miracle in my body. We discussed how we desired the miracle to unfold in GOD's design, impacting the most lives. Of course, I would relish my healing be completed already. However, if GOD's providence is to weave a path for me that touches many lives and transforms hearts, so be it. GOD's plan is always best.

Stephanie and I pulled up to our hotel and opened the door to our room, immediately noticing a basket of goodies and card on our bed. I assumed it was a mistake or a pay as you take stash. It turned out to be a heartfelt gift from my co-worker whom I had spent time with praising GOD. He called the hotel I mentioned we were staying at and requested the gift basket. The most cherished item was the card. Written within were the words "Escapes from death belong to the LORD!" We shed tears of joy and embraced. GOD was choosing such a gentle and encouraging path for us.

We gazed out our window upon Inner Harbor and noticed an outdoor concert venue below our window. It was clear many people were arriving for an evening concert. I wondered what band would be providing us some free music for the evening. I looked up the venue and date online and let out a joyful laugh. This concert could have been any genre or artist, but tonight it was two Christian bands! How perfect, another birthday gift I thought. Switchfoot and Lighthouse would be singing for the glory of the LORD and we could delight in the concert.

With the concert about to start, we decided to forgo dining at an upscale restaurant. Instead, we purchased some food we could eat sitting outside. This would allow us to take joy in the music and embrace the charm of the harbor. We returned with our meals and settled in a comfortable spot. Stephanie and I glanced down the pier and clear as day was a man wearing a Superman T-shirt. We again felt moved. GOD certainly orchestrated a memorable evening for us.

Our evening continued to be blessed beyond measure. We noticed an attractive young couple and their children enjoying the harbor near us. They also appeared to enjoy the music and engaged with us in conversation. It was their daughter's birthday and they traveled to the harbor at her request. Our conversations were pleasant, yet we sensed GOD had arranged this encounter. We were not sure what his heart was for the meeting.

We all relaxed delighting in the concert. A moment arrived where the singer paused and shouted we need to sing happy birthday for one of our band members. This was perfect. This young girl and I were serenaded (in our opinions) happy birthday by thousands of people attending the concert. The conversation continued, and we discovered the heart behind our divine encounter. It turned out they had a parent impacted by prostate cancer. We had a chance to share our journey so far, testifying of GOD's hand and my healing diet. It was undoubtedly a divine moment. It caused me to consider how GOD weaves people, places and time creating a master tapestry. I imagined GOD influencing all things for those who love him even painting beauty with ashes. My comprehension of our world and suffering is certainly deficient, but I recognize GOD loves us and partakes in our burdens. At that moment, I understood that if I perceived the fullness of what GOD knows about situations, I would choose the exact path he does. I believe GOD chooses the way that delivers the most love to situations without revoking our free will.

We peacefully strolled to our hotel for the night, I thanked GOD for an awe-inspiring birthday. I shared with GOD how I loved experiencing him so frequently in my day to day. I expressed I longed for his grace to help me to continue a life with eyes and ears wide open, anticipating his involvement and awareness of his presence.

August 16, 2017

I woke up anticipating more moments with GOD today during our Hopkins visit. Stephanie and I drove to the hospital arriving much earlier than our appointment time. In a lobby situated outside of the oncology waiting room was a beautiful grand piano, artwork and seating areas.

I chose to sit down at the piano and create some music from my heart. A few people gave me thumbs up or stopped and listened for a few moments before continuing. I sensed GOD's anointing in my playing. As I continued, a lady approached and proclaimed she felt GOD's spirit all over the music I was playing. She was in tears and shared her daughter was currently in surgery for cancer, she now believed everything was going to be alright. I agreed with an amen.

My time to visit with a medical team arrived. I shared the T-shirt concept and all I was doing in respects to diet and faith. The team was pleased we were upbeat, but I could read uncertainty in their body language. Stephanie whispered, *"The team seemed very excited when we came in the room. It was as if they somehow know you're getting the real drug not the placebo."*

After this medical meeting, we had a sidebar with the clinical trial nurse and advised her we wanted to skip "chemo class". In chemo class, you learn about all the possible side effect and how to handle them. We explained to her how important words had become to us and we would rather deal with any side effects as they come rather than imagine and fear them. At first, she was hesitant but conceded we could skip the class. She told us the trial drug would be prepared shortly and that we could wait in the lobby. She noted, *"Let's meet at the piano."*

Some time passed, and I received a three-month supply of the trial drug. Stephanie and I believed without a doubt I had the real thing. We thanked GOD for leading us, taking care of us and this additional birthday present; the next generation of treatment. Chemotherapy dates were now on the calendar. I would receive an infusion once every three weeks also returning for blood work each week after treatment. I was to become a frequent visitor to the hospital.

August 17, 2017

Back to work but I was expectant. Not only for my health but I was growing closer to GOD. I spent a bit of time talking with a co-worker and sharing how Stephanie and I planned to wear positive T-shirts for each Hopkins visit. She felt this was an amazing idea and offered to buy shirts for us. She also declared, *"I bet others here at work would do the same."*

"That is an amazing idea, but I may go a slightly different direction." I decided to reach out to a Christian T-shirt company Kerusso and share our vision, asking if they were interested in donating any T-shirts. I contacted them via a link on their website and sent my email. It was not guaranteed I would even get a response, they might get hit up all day long with requests or perhaps I would get a polite sorry.

A few hours later I received a response. It was from Lori. She herself was a stage 4 lymphoma survivor and she loved the idea. Lori said she would see the idea moved up the ladder for consideration. Once again GOD's love and faithfulness overwhelmed me. Not only did I receive a faith boost hearing from a stage 4 survivor, but I sensed he was going to provide some help for us with the T-shirts for Hopkins.

August 18-19, 2017

One of the areas I remained compelled to improve was fitness. Embracing the wisdom; improved fitness equates to improved health I endeavored to do more. I left work a bit early and drove to the YMCA. I met with Steve a programs director and completed an intake application joining a program for cancer patients and survivors. This program Livestrong is quite remarkable. Through Livestrong and their partnership with the Y, participants are provided twelve weeks of support and training. This training goes far beyond simply working out. Participants receive individualized exercise routines based on their capabilities along with personal training. Members encourage one another sharing hope. Being part of this group also inspires you to show up even on the days your mind or body doesn't want to. Steve the group leader and I had an instant connection, we both shared a passion for the power of food and what we allow our minds to believe.

This would be the last weekend prior to chemo. Fully aware of this, we planned a getaway with our children, my sister, and her daughter. We traveled to Gettysburg and stayed in a handsome Civil War themed hotel. We came up with activities to enjoy our moments together. Some of these were successfully completing an escape room, hot tub and pool time, card games and plenty of laughs and hugs.

Both nights I had a curious thing occur. I awoke suddenly and fully, gazing at the alarm clock. Both nights the clock displayed the identical time 12:12. Is this important, something I need to notice GOD? I was uncertain but made a note in my journal assuming I may understand more in the future.

Returning home Sunday evening I decided to pre-plan and practice a visualization for the first chemo treatment. I conceived a personalized visualization. My game plan was to imagine my healthy cells appearing as the Superman symbol completely impervious to damage. The cancer cells would be fragile as butter and the chemo a blazing radiant light. During my practice session, I envisioned the chemo starting in my vein slowly proceeding to circulate through my body liquefying any and all cancer cells, causing zero destruction to my healthy cells. I was pleased with this plan and felt prepared for the upcoming chemo infusion.

August 20, 2017

I awoke from another vivid dream, on the clock again was 12:12. My dream was of my mother speaking to me *"Shawn, you know that tree you told me about. Think of it not as a fruit tree but as a root tree."* There were some obvious associations I could deduce, however, what did I need to understand from this? All that came to mind was; any genuine fruit in our lives originates from healthy roots. I prayed may you always remain my root LORD.

Treasure from
the Darkness

*God weaves our lives in and out of others, often we cross
paths for a reason. Don't miss divine connections.*

Chemo

August 21, 2017

I had a couple of days of work to endure before chemo. I arrived at work and made my way to my office. Sitting on my desk was an envelope. The moment I opened it, I grasped how beloved of GOD I was. A perfect artisan created card adorned with the letters LIFE was in my hands. It was from the administration department; a picture of their entire team cheering me on graced the body of the card. Beyond this treasure itself, they purchased me a gift card to a local grocery store understanding healthy food was now so significant to me.

August 22, 2017

Today was the eve before chemo round number one. Stephanie arranged for friends to meet with us for an intimate evening prayer time. This gathering was at Life Center, in their prayer room known as the "furnace". The atmosphere was filled with worship and everyone was of one heart seeking GOD's face and mercy. At one point, I laid on the floor resting and praying. An image filled my mind. In the vision, Stephanie and I were mounted on horses adorned for battle.

All I could see initially was these powerful mounts and us. I expected we were about to be thrust into a battlefield. Instead, as my gaze moved outward, in front of us was peaceful grassland adjacent to a sandy beach. Gracefully we road together as gentle waves rolled in. My mind processed the vision I was seeing. Does this mean our journey will not be a vicious battle? Is the path before us a peaceful one?

During our drive home, my mom called and shared an encounter she experienced earlier in the day. She ran into a lady from church who was diligently praying for me. She told my mom she was no longer wearing her "pray for Shawn" bracelet, she felt GOD told her during prayer time I was going to be OK. I was moved by the entire evening yet still I longed to hear words of life from the doctors.

August 23, 2017

Up at 4 am but that was fine, sleep was not possible. Today was my first chemo infusion. My son Josiah awoke at his house at 3 am and drove an hour to be our chauffeur for the day. My heart was beating with confidence in GOD's healing power and expecting our shirts and their messages of hope to inspire.

We traveled to Hopkins arriving early, my blood work was started by 7 am. After the labs, I made my way to the piano in their lobby again and played. One of the Hopkins greeters walked over and said, *"Thank you so much for playing. It would be great to have someone playing all the time."*

It would take some time for my infusion to be prepared, so we trekked around the hospital. We discovered a wall giving tribute to the breakthroughs at Hopkins over the years. Nearby were banners declaring Hopkins the number one hospital in the world for twenty straight years, slipping ever so slightly this year to number three.

A special tribute honoring Johns Hopkins the man grabbed my attention. I read both his biography and the history of the hospital.

Johns Hopkins was the first hospital/university combination, greatly influencing medicine in the modern age. Part of the biography stated Johns Hopkins was a Quaker and immediately I had a thought "I bet this wasn't his idea alone, I bet GOD entrusted him how to bequeath his fortune!" I determined this was a mystery I must investigate later.

It was time to receive the infusion. I chose a location near a window that allowed me to lie down. The IV was inserted into my vein and medication began to drip. Would I feel a sensation as it entered my blood? Would I become ill to my stomach as so many do? My understanding was chemo nausea largely occurs because chemo works by killing fast-growing cells. One of the locations in the body with fast-growing cells is the stomach. The chemo kills cells of the stomach lining and healthy gut bacteria. I planned to eat probiotic and high fiber foods every day in hopes of avoiding stomach problems.

For several days before the infusion, I had been practicing my visualization. Today was the real deal. I had my headphones on, tuned into worship music and I started my pre-planned visualization. Surprisingly, shortly after starting my pre-planned imagery the pictures in my mind transformed. No longer was I seeing the chemo melting cancer cells and my healthy cells protected.

Instead, I beheld a massive magnet seated under a conveyor belt. Cancer cells were being pulled to the end of this belt and being melted into nothingness. After some time visualizing this, the conveyor transformed in shape becoming circular. It was rotating rapidly. Tiny particles like grains of salt were being pulled from all directions within my body. As the particles landed they were obliterated. I reasoned in my mind, what on earth is happening? In my heart, I heard, *"Those are the stem cells."* I had never imagined any of this or even considered cancer stem cells.

The treatment time passed quickly. I was invigorated by the vision I was gifted. I removed my headphones and chatted with

Stephanie. I told her I sensed we need to trust GOD's time table with the medical staff and chose to not get frustrated by delays or changes. I knew GOD was orchestrating all the moving parts of this journey even when we could not see it. On our trip home I revealed what had happened during my treatment with Stephanie and Josiah.

August 24, 2017

The morning after my first chemo treatment I woke up feeling nothing but peace. I decided I would go to work as I was feeling well. I received an email from Lori at Kerusso their management loved our idea and they would be donating some positive message T-shirts. My thought life was doing well 95% of the time. I was bursting with faith and expecting abundant life. The remaining 5% of the time when fear came knocking I was quick at kicking it out.

The first post-chemo weekend rolled in and I experienced some fatigue. In matching magnitude as my fatigue increased so did my mental struggles. Do I know GOD's will for my life? Does he plan for me to live? What if his plans include me dying? Fear was persistent in hitting me during this weakened state, but GOD was near and allowed me to find peace and faith.

A difficult moment for us between chemo weeks… Stephanie's words:

August 25-27, 2017

"I am not going in there with you."

I did not want to go in either. We pulled up to the store near our house. I needed to buy a sympathy card for a friend that lost her Grandfather. My friend and her husband attended my Dad's Service not too long ago. I wanted to make sure she knew I was thinking of them at this time.

I was trembling when I set foot towards the sympathy card section in the store. I read Loss of Father, Loss of Mother, Loss of Wife, Loss of Husband, etc. I wanted to cry… just cry. Fear was trying to ooze into my being, it wanted to swallow me up in the sympathy cards, especially the ones that were screaming loss of Husband.

I made a rather quick choice because I did not want to be there much longer. I felt tears welling up inside me. When I got back into the car, I told Shawn that was awful. He said that is why I did not want to go in there with you. I became wobbly and I did not want to imagine Loss of Husband cards mailed to me at the end of this.

We pulled out of the parking lot onto the highway and began the drive to a friend's house for dinner. Shawn merged over to the left lane on 83 North. The left lane is the fast lane, yet, traffic seemed to be moving slower in the left lane at that point. I was gazing out the passenger side window trying to pull myself together from the experience in the card store. Suddenly, a black pick-up truck passed us on the right side where I could clearly read what was displayed on the back window of the truck. There it was! In vibrant gold lettering the Superman symbol on the rear window of the pick-up truck.

Now, I really started to cry. The perfect timing of this truck driving by was a personal loving sign from GOD. I knew with all my heart GOD sent that truck at that moment to lift me up and get me back on the life path… His Promise of Life! A gold symbol from

Heaven, His Glory, His Promise, that *this* was true... that we would remain in life!

I'm crying now as I remember the experience... only He can do something like that! He loves His Children!

Treasure from
the Darkness

*Don't think every dream or vision is bad pizza;
journal these events even when they do not make sense
in the moment.*

Running

September 1, 2017

One of the difficult realities of a cancer journey is it also attacks your bank account. GOD was moving hearts to help us with this. I was blessed today with an unexpected financial gift of $1,200 to assist with my medical bills. The gift filled me with thankfulness. My needs were being met and I had not asked for financial help.

September 2, 2017

Josiah popped in for a visit. He assisted us hanging a wall decoration my parents purchased for us. It reads, "Fear not tomorrow GOD is already there". Its words encourage me, not a single circumstance about my life or situation is a surprise to GOD. My story is already written. I simply must align my heart with his.

We were invited by Bob Stahl to join a service "healing tree international" hosts Saturday evenings. We were uncertain what to expect but recognized Bob and the healing room prayer team as part of our journey. We agreed to be there. When we arrived, Bob shared their leadership team had already had a session introducing the theme of the service. The guest speaker's topic was trauma and how more times than not there are roots that cause the fruits. Meaning of course, the outward symptoms and behaviors are driven by deeper heart issues. I chuckled and mentioned the dream of my mother. I continued telling Bob of my breakthrough moment renouncing fear as the commanding emotion of my life.

During worship, a lady from across the room marched towards me and plopped in the empty chair beside me. She articulated that GOD had her bring special anointing oil for this evening. She proceeded to share She knew in her heart, GOD would reveal who it was meant for tonight. That somebody was me. She proceeded to reveal this oil accumulated and was bottled from a Moravian bible that continually is secreting oil. This oil she voiced has been used to anoint others and they received healing. I accepted this gift, allowing her to pour the oil over my head praying for my healing.

After the sermon, Abby the leader was furthering an atmosphere of ministry. Abby asked me to rise and share with the group my story thus far. I declared to the group I am on a healing journey and testified what GOD has already done. I declared, *"I have not seen the healing yet, but know it is happening."* After the ministry time, many people came over to speak with me. A few people asked me to pray with them for their healing. Others wanted to encourage me. One gentleman revealed, while I was on the stage he envisioned two waves crashing over me, first a wave made of fire and the second wave water. He declared he has no doubt GOD is healing me. Another gentleman who prayed for me during my first visit to the healing rooms whispered to me through his tears. He shared he just had his PSA checked and the results were less than 0.1. Upon receiving this number, he declared in prayer the same results for me. One lady I noticed standing nearby wanted to talk with me but had to leave. I would later learn what she wanted to share.

On the drive home I was feeling refreshed and overjoyed we had attended the service. I invested my late evening hours research-ing Johns Hopkin's life and the Quaker faith. I discovered Quakers during worship dedicate time to simply sit in silence waiting on GOD to meet them. I imagined Johns Hopkins doing this very thing, asking GOD for wisdom with his wealth. GOD responding with a vision of a legacy. I pondered in my mind, what the actual will he left indicated. I located information about his will and a letter of his last wishes and read through it. The documents blueprinted the creation of the hos-pital and university and much more. His final wishes left money to educate women in nursing a new idea in that day, funds for the care of the poor and a declaration of his desire that within the hospital administration there was to be a place made for GOD. Bingo! The im-pression I had may be right. I located further testimonials and articles where people including John's Hopkin's gardener reflected on his life. They mentioned Johns would share with others his wealth was not his, but something he was a steward over. I felt inspired to pray for Johns Hopkins Hospital, for breakthroughs in healing technologies and that fruit would multiply from the seeds planted. May the roots of this tree bring fruit transforming how healing takes place in the world.

September 3, 2017

Service at Life Center was once again uplifting. I tithed despite the financial pressures recently increasing. Stephanie and I made our way to the altar for post-service prayer again. The couple praying for us sensed a roller coaster with some ups and downs but said you don't stay down for long. They continued, *"This will come to a finish line and be done soon. Your healing is coming. It is not your time; you have more to do and more to live. He loves you so very much."* Wow, one more valiant prayer. Thank you GOD, all these prayers and visions are ex-actly what my heart longs to hear.

September 4-8, 2017

This week was steady as she goes. I stayed the course, healthy eating, exercise, prayer time, and research into health. I learned that certain foods can act as PARP inhibitors, a cutting-edge cancer therapy for those with gene defective forms. Wow, the first oncologist had said to eat whatever you want, GOD whispered healing is in the garden. My daddy GOD certainly knows everything about me and graciously led me to food as part of my healing.

I received a call from Bob Stahl sharing a lady at the healing tree meeting confided in him while I was sharing, she saw a huge healing angel standing behind me on the stage. I was overwhelmed by the idea of angels being assigned on my behalf.

A package arrived with T-shirts from Kerusso blessed for our next Hopkins visit. The messages were not pre-known to us. Both T-shirts bore a declaration of faith. We will be wearing these to chemo number two. I longed to have a lab to test my own PSA number. I imagined my number was already dropping to zero, GOD's healing was flowing through me.

September 9-10, 2017

A highlight of our weekend was dinner with Jessica and Johnathan. They had traversed a cancer journey themselves. We discussed faith, diet, and medicine. We learned they were involved in a drug trial that now was the standard of care and part of my treatment protocol. This connection was encouraging for all of us.

At church, I received more encouraging words I saved in my journal. One friend boldly said, *"I feel like Shawn may already be healed but he is in this trial for the sake of the other men."* I thought to myself, so be it. I will endure chemo treatments and any struggles associated with it even if it is for the sake of others. Please let it be that my healing helps this trial move forward allowing this new medication to be fast-tracked. Another friend said, *"God has given you wisdom and the mind to do research on diet and supplements and you will someday help others who could not do these themselves."*

September 11-13, 2017

Normal days leading up to my next chemo. Pre-chemo blood counts returned, I was at all normal levels. Seeing this made me smile. I knew in my heart the prayers and my diet was giving me the edge. I again found myself at the piano in the lobby and played worship songs from the heart. Many friends asked Steph to share a video clip of me playing on Facebook. Stephanie posted a short video and I could not believe how many views popped up. I perhaps expected ten or twenty. Quickly the number grew to almost a thousand views. I pondered in my heart the people beholding this healing journey. From the start, we have been declaring faith and GOD's power to heal. Please GOD, honor our faith and declarations I do not want to bring shame to your name. My mind briefly entertained an image of me dying and Stephanie being left alone, not only missing a husband but struggling and embarrassed of her faith. This was such a disturbing contemplation my heart ached. The two dearest parts of my life, my wife and my GOD were being used to assault my mind.

My infusion nurse resembled a beloved friend of ours. This chance occurrence provided me some comfort. As the chemo infusion started, I adorned my headphones tuning in Pandora worship. I asked GOD to be with me during the treatment. I began visualizing my body being cleansed of any remaining cancer cells. Surprisingly and suddenly my mind shifted, and I was fearful. My thought life had been strong recently, and GOD continually was showing his grace. Why was I fighting fear again? My thoughts somehow got hijacked, I perceived a voice in my mind yelling at me. The voice screamed I was delusional for my faith and what I should be doing is planning my end of life arrangements. I did not open my eyes and express this nightmare with Stephanie, instead, I cried out to GOD with my heart of hearts pleading for him to rescue me. At that precise moment, I experienced a wave of love and comfort as a divine song began to play. The song was one I never heard before. It was "I Am Not Alone" by Kari Jobe. Tears rolled as I felt GOD himself was embedding this song into my heart. The fear completely vanished, and my mind envisioned Stephanie and I traveling, sharing our testimony of GOD's faithfulness, love and healing power. I recalled the lesson the spirit delivered during an earlier battle with fear. If a thought comes with fear attached, it is not from GOD. Once the infusion was complete, I shared with Stephanie the song and how near GOD was to us.

My days after this chemo treatment were filled with fatigue. My stomach did well, and I did not struggle with the predicted nausea. I believe this was in part due to diet efforts keeping up good stomach bacteria. My mother is so wonderful. Each day she made homemade meals with vegetables, legumes, fruits, nuts, and mushrooms loaded with healing properties. Even though she often worked with unfamiliar combinations, she managed to create appetizing meals.

September 14-22, 2017

Despite chemotherapy treatments, life was improving daily. I was working normal days, my mind was focused on GOD's faithfulness, healthy nutrition, and love for my family. My heart stayed very close to GOD this week and my grasp of what matters in life was becoming clearer. I pondered what it means to seek GOD with all your heart. Could I or anyone truly do this? I want to… but my human fleshly nature is like a zombie that never dies completely. I reasoned I am a work in progress and as I die more to myself, I will know GOD more.

I pulled into a parking lot of a local grocery store heading home from work. I found myself feeling frustrated with people I observed not being courteous to others. As I began to quietly judge them in my heart and mind, I felt a nudge in my spirit say, *"People are not obstacles."* I immediately saw the situation with new eyes. All these people are GOD's children and he loves them dearly. They too are in battles with their flesh. Some are in fact completely blind and in bondage to a life that never sees beyond the natural. I asked GOD to give me more of his heart for my fellow man.

The day of the cancer walk arrived. I was both excited and nervous. The night was unseasonably hot and yet over six hundred participants were ready to run. A large group of family and friends were with me. In addition, my work had a large team supporting me. My family and friend team all came wearing Superman shirts. I assumed the emotion I ought to feel was love. Somehow, I had the feeling I needed to be a host, assuring all the guests were comfortable and taken care of.

I found myself pre-race struggling to know what appropriate behavior was. I perceived I had an obligation to thank every person individually for their support. This responsibility kept me running around. Beyond the two teams supporting me, there were other people I wanted to speak with. I caught a glimpse of the office manager who lingered after normal business hours. Shawn Supers the Mid Atlantic Director and MC for the event. I found the strength to calm myself down and engaged in one meaningful conversation at a time.

Now that my mind was calm, my emotions returned to love and hope. Running together with six hundred other people determined to witness the end of cancer is heartwarming. Occasionally I would notice a shirt or sign in memory of a loved one who lost their fight. I knew this was a reality, but it still troubled me. I completed the run, hot, tired, and satisfied. After the majority of participants had completed the race, a ceremony was held. The climax of the ceremony recognized survivors and caregivers. This portion was an emotional whirlwind. In the survivor's and caregiver's faces, I saw fear, pain, hope, courage, and victory all jumbled together. A singer Jimmy Charles was performing, he sang a song he wrote about cancer titled "Superman". Wow, how is this possible? I never in a million years could have planned this. Team Super Shawn, Shawn Supers and now the song Superman. GOD was near and weaving messages of hope into this journey.

After the event I found a moment to speak with Shawn Supers and share how well I was doing along with some of the events that had occurred in my life since diagnosis. She exclaimed, *"Wow perhaps we should get you to be our main speaker next year."* Processing what she just said my heart was conflicted, my faith declared yes. Reason retorted you are still in treatments for the most advanced state of cancer and somehow, you're going to speak courage to others? I shook off the negative voice and declared in my heart I would be healed by next year and share my story.

Treasure from
the Darkness

*True hope comes from knowing God has always
been and always will be faithful.*

It's Worth the Climb

I was sensing my health and thought life was stronger than early in the journey. I was having many spiritual and healing focused dreams. One dream encouraged me greatly. In my dream, I was able to see and examine my skeletal system. My bones were healed and cancer free and they were being buffed by some sort of helper cells to a shiny glimmer. I woke up the morning after this dream feeling confident about my future.

Not every dream during this season was pleasant. In fact, I had a very disturbing dream that haunted me for a few days. In this dream, I was viewing scenes of myself at a youth retreat. The place in my dream was from a distant memory. I was sitting on the floor participating as I would have in my youth days. I noticed some men in the room and immediately knew they were not good. One of the men approached me handing me a two-way radio. He whispered, *"Keep this with you, we have an offer for you."* The whole scenario was very uncomfortable but for some reason, I took the radio. Eventually, my dream shifted to a setting where I was alone, and a voice came across the radio. The voice barked, *"We know about your cancer, and know how you can be healed. We have a deal for you."* The strangest part was they mentioned a type of cancer I was not even diagnosed with. Even in my dream, I knew GOD would not be making deals with me on healing. I woke up feeling horrible and confused.

A few days past and I continued to be troubled by this dream. I decided I needed another visit to the healing room at Life Center seeking prayer. I was thrilled to visit again and provide positive updates to people praying so fervently for me. After the updates I told the team, I have this dream eating at me the last few days. I shared the entire dream in detail. The team decided to pray about it. My spirit immediately jumped when one of those praying shared. *"Shawn, I feel like God is saying to me there is no other deal but Life!"* The confusion and turmoil I carried for days melted off me instantly. A few others chimed in, sharing what they felt in their hearts. One voiced they had an impression I was surrounded by angels and GOD was giving me downloads of wisdom. Another said I keep feeling the answer was already given "Yes" and that I was healed.

What an amazing prayer time, such positive words of faith and hope. If GOD decrees I am healed and there is no other deal but life. It most certainly is as he has said.

October 1, 2017

I invested some time reflecting on all I was experiencing in this season of life. I was overwhelmed by the many recent supernatural experiences. As I thought about my life pre-diagnosis, I realized I often felt alone. I accepted in my heart of hearts, my life's purpose was limited to going to work and loving my family. Now during this dark struggle in life, GOD was moving people's hearts to show genuine love for me. My family was loving and helping with food and practical needs. My spiritual family including my physical family were holding me in prayer daily.

I began to perceive a picture in my mind of their faith and love. I was comparable to the paralyzed man on his bed lowered through the roof of a building placed at the feet of Jesus. As I lay there in the loving gaze of my creator, I understand the depth of his love and forgiveness. As desperately as I need to be physically healed, that is my secondary need. What I need above all else is to know my savior and rest at his feet. As my mind ponders deeper. I begin to process some "what ifs" and pursuits of the heart of man. "What if" I was the wealthiest person of all time? Of course, I would have no cares I thought. I could do whatever, whenever I wanted. I could enjoy great pleasures and do extravagant deeds of kindness. I then imagined the end of life for that existence. What would matter? My heart weighed the situation and concluded. All that would have worth is; did I give GOD 100% of my life and heart. Did I share his light and love with everyone I was given the chance? Did I seek and know my savior, living for him, his pleasure and purpose?

I continued this line of thinking to another common desire, a thirst for power or influence during one's life. I considered the most renowned rulers of men and their eventual demise. I pondered not only their lives but their empires or achievements. Even the greatest endeavors of man are temporal. Many scenarios rolled through my mind. I imagined the conclusions I was reaching were like Solomon's when he concluded: *"This too is meaningless."*

I measured my own heart. I want to know my LORD and never stop growing in him. I also yearn to fulfill a purpose during my life. My purpose does not need to be exalted or honored by the world; it can be just between GOD and me. I suddenly snapped out this dreamlike state. It was as if I had been sleepwalking through years of my life. I prayed, *"God I will never say no, teach me and lead me into what I was made to be."* After this prayer, I began to understand GOD is in everything we do, not just triumphant achievements. I will "live well" the days, opportunities and breaths I have been given. I will preserve my heart and spirit for his leading, even if it is a single step at a time.

October 2-8, 2017

Chemo week arrived again. Stephanie and I carefully chose positive shirts to wear this week, the message we decided upon was "GOD's Love". As we strolled the halls of the hospital, we noticed many pairs of eyes drawn to the life-giving messages. Yes, these were merely T-shirts, however, they carried power. Their power was derived from the words. Words change hearts. Words change nations. Words change everything.

For this chemo treatment, I once again popped on headphones turning on praise and worship music. I closed my eyes and prepared to visualize the chemo traveling through my system hunting down any remaining or hidden cancer cells. Once again, my pre-planned visualization took a surprise detour. As I pictured the chemo flowing through my system no cancer cells were located. Instead, what I saw in my mind's eye was my bones and locations pointed out in past scans. These areas were now being buffed to a shiny glimmer. It was exactly like the dream I had a few days earlier. Wow, what a miraculous vision to have. I experienced such peace wash over me, I dedicated the remaining treatment time to pray for others I knew were braving cancer journeys.

The remainder of this week burdened us with torturous challenges created by our daughter's life choices. Despite the fact she was sprinting full speed and head first into sin, we saw GOD's mercy. GOD was merciful and gave us a little wink from heaven. On our way to church, Stephanie and I discussed our daughter's life choices and disregard for everything she was taught in her life. I blurted out in frustration *"I don't even know what to do anymore. If I knew what I could do I would do it!"* As those words fell out of my mouth a large tractor-trailer rolled passed us, on the back doors in large letters was written "Trust GOD". I laughed, pointed and declared, *"Well except that!"* Stephanie and I thanked GOD for these words of hope. We confessed this challenge was beyond us, but we would trust GOD has her life too.

October 9-10, 2017

The weekend after this chemo treatment, I weathered a few side effects. My taste buds took a vacation making everything taste like metal. I had fatigue beyond what I would consider normal. I tolerated these challenges and acknowledged a truth, it is more challenging to keep your mind positive while your body is depleted. Amidst the heaviness, I was impressed to read a tale of Elisha. Elisha was encircled by a massive army. His servant seeing the army, grew full of fear. Elisha pronounced, *"Don't be afraid, those who are with us are more than those who are with them."* GOD empowered the servant to see the angel armies far outnumbering the earthy forces. I reflected on all the prayers surrounding me and declared in my weakened state, *"More are with me than against me."*

I became fascinated with the concept of seeing things as they are and not merely as I perceive them. I prayed to ask GOD for better vision of the world around me and help to remember to seek the truth about things that may be veiled to the eye.

October 11-18, 2017

My body swiftly bounced back from this trying chemo round. Blood work numbers indicated my immune system was rebuilding exceptionally fast. Beyond time invested in researching foods I investigated current and future therapies for cancer. I discovered a new study that indicated the use of an earlier generation AR antagonist along with the ADT and chemo greatly extended men's lives and was now being fast track approved as a combination therapy. This was excellent news for me. Combination therapy was already the approach of the trial I was on and I had the benefit of a next-generation AR antagonist not even on the market yet. I recognized GOD opened the doors leading me to Hopkins and this trial.

I deliberated a bit on the fact that many people choose a side when it comes to treatments. Some go full holistic and view powerful chemical therapies as poison. Others boldly declare holistic approaches are quackery. My impression is that there are benefits to both healing approaches. In most cases, a treatment protocol that incorporates both with the addition of faith will achieve the best outcomes.

October 19-29, 2017

Stephanie and I were in a good place in our hearts. We looked forward to our moments together each day after work. We ventured outdoors to a community park where we walked and talked. Every night we would repeat the promises of life GOD was imparting to us and enjoy vigorous walks. My studies into nutrition were significantly increasing my understanding of food and its actions within the human body. I felt my faith rising and I was declaring to others, including health professionals, *"I am healed! You just haven't seen it yet."* Some nodded out of kindness while others I could see struggled with my declaration perhaps desiring to tell me that they thought I was delusional.

I was heading into chemo round four and the infusion nurses mentioned, *"I hear you are just sailing through this."*

The doctor shared another PSA test would be done in November, even though I am still receiving chemo rounds. I was not fearful, instead, I was excited. I declared my expectation of a fantastic number.

I asked GOD for a great number, *"Please let it display the work you are doing in me to the medical community."* I had zero side effects from this round of chemo, in fact, I could tell I was becoming stronger and healthier every day.

A moment Stephanie captured in words during our journey:

Flat Rock Hike in Newville, Pennsylvania.

We decided once Shawn recovered from his recent round of chemo treatment, we would go on a hike in the mountains and enjoy the autumn beauty. We wanted to celebrate getting past the half-way point of Shawn's treatments and get outdoors. We looked forward to the fresh air, an escape, exercise, beauty, and feeling close to GOD and his creation.

We pulled into the park. The scenery was draped with campers, streams of water, vibrant trees, campfires, pavilions, and the inviting trails that attract hikers. The trail whispered to our spirits come up here...

We finished our coffee and the bees followed us to the restroom facility before we got started. The air was a halo of campfire and burdens were tumbling down the streams of water as people were in relax mode.

The start point gave us two choices for the hike up, either an easy start or a challenging start. We chose the challenge... we did not know what that was going to entail.

The climb was steep, rocky, our legs were screaming, hearts pounding, breathing accelerated, and we had to make several stops along the way to rest and catch our breath. We took moments to hydrate, nibble on snacks we packed, and take in the surroundings.

Those making their trip down would say such things like, *"Keep going the view is worth it, you still have a long way to go, we know exactly how you are feeling, but it is worth it... We promise..."*

We were definitely on a challenging steep made for Olympian caliber. I was amazed at Shawn's determination to keep climbing under those circumstances and the fact he was under treatment that weakens and fatigues the body. He was sweating and his heart rate was up too. I kept pushing snacks, water, and breaks. At one point there was a break in the climb. A flat walk. It was absolutely gorgeous. The trees were majestic and the breeze sent dancing leaves down upon us like blessings. Sunbeams flooded the earth from the heavens and we stood in them and absorbed the light. We felt His Presence.

Then the climbing started again. We thought we were getting closer, yet, that was not the case, again hikers coming down said to keep going it is worth it. We were hot, sweaty, growing tired, and wonder if we would ever make it to the top. I kept thinking to myself, Shawn is relentless, determined, a fighter, look at him go. These passer-byes have no idea what we are going through and we are making this climb because we heard the view is worth it.

Finally, we arrived at the very top of the mountain. Hikers have been up and down from that spot. When we arrived there was no one there. We were given a holy moment. A moment that overwhelmed Shawn with tears of joy! The beauty overtook him and he couldn't help but cry. The moment was powerful, eagles were flying near us, the view far exceeded our expectations. We gazed upon farmlands, fields, meadows, and a mountain range on the other side staring back at us, trees below us, and a holy silence hovered over the view. There are no words to describe what it was like for us. We felt His Presence, His Promises, His Love, and He met us there at that moment before the other hikers made their way next to us.

October 30-November 5, 2017

What a joy it is to encourage someone else's faith. I witnessed the faith of others rising due to our journey. Everyone I would spend time in conversation with expected nothing short of a miracle. What was particularly amazing is this extended beyond people I would expect to believe. Quite a few seekers were repeating, there is a miracle happening in my life, everyone sees it. As terrible as cancer is, I was overjoyed I was being used by GOD.

GOD brought to light a new area where growth was needed. So often I was quick to get stressed by situations where I was slowed down such as crowds and traffic. I asked GOD to teach me to find peace in these little insignificant challenges of life. Why did I allow things like this to bother me? I pondered for a moment and realized, I would rather sit for five years in a traffic jam with Stephanie than be without her. GOD is molding my heart and restoring the damage I have done to myself by living in my own understanding.

Treasure from
the Darkness

The view at the top is worth the climb.

Not Only About Me

November 8, 2017

November 8 arrived; today I would receive a clinical blood marker detailing what was taking place inside me. I would also be given my normal lab work including an EKG. Some lab results take longer to be processed and uploaded for review than others. Once all the tests were completed, I made my way to the parking garage and started the journey home. I was anticipating as the day proceeded the varied lab results would pop up for my review. I was only a few miles from the hospital and my phone rang. It was my clinical trial nurse. She calmly but firmly said, *"Shawn I need you to come back right away and meet me in the emergency room."*

Surprisingly, my EKG results were abnormal. I could not fathom why I was heading into the ER for heart exams. I felt fantastic, I prayed "What is this about?" I was reminded of a commitment I made earlier. I would not get frustrated by changes and delays in my care. I would trust GOD is moving all the pieces.

I made my way to the ER and was greeted by my nurse. She explained I needed to undergo heart tests based upon the EKG. I spent hours in the ER receiving a full battery of different tests. The entire time my clinical trial nurse stayed right beside me. This situation was obviously concerning for the trial, they would not want any adverse events associated with the new drug.

My nurse and I endured considerable down times between tests. We used this time to chat about my journey and what GOD was doing in my life. She confided to me in the past, she would pray for patients as she walked the halls, but due to repeat disappointments she no longer does. I could see in her face she lost faith that prayer helped patients. Inside I experienced a rush of courage and understood the purpose of spending a day in the ER. I conveyed to her *"I think I know why we are here together today. You need to pray again for patients. It does matter. Look at what is taking place in my body! At times you may be the only one praying for someone."*

A moment later, the cancer blood lab uploaded to my chart. I logged into the system via my phone to review the report. My blood marker returned as (0.2). This is an almost undetectable number. The magic number is (<0.1). However, my marker moved significantly in the right direction and was close to undetectable. The nurse was excited, *"That is a great number! It is almost undetectable."*

I declared, *"It is God healing me, through the combination of my care here, my food and prayers."*

An ER nurse walked in on us, *"We have no idea why you had an abnormal EKG earlier. All the labs and heart studies have come back completely normal."*

I smiled, *"That is exactly what I expected to hear. Thank you so much for your help today."* I was now free to drive home. I used the travel time to rejoice and share the testimony of the day with others.

At home, Stephanie and I praised GOD for the amazing number and asked GOD to complete his work in me. I explained to Stephanie this is a good number but not complete. If that marker lingered above 0.1 cancer remained in my system. I knew GOD had me in his hands.

November 9-20, 2017

A few days had passed since my PSA lab. I was munching down on a healthy breakfast and my phone vibrated. An email arrived indicating a new lab report uploaded to my chart. I felt a wave of nervousness as I didn't expect any additional labs. I logged in to discover what this could be. It turned out Hopkins uploaded the labs performed by the trial drug company to my personal chart. The pharmaceutical company also completed a PSA lab. Their report hit me with a wave of emotion. The report listed my PSA as (0.13) their lab measured results to an additional decimal place. I was so near the desired (0.1). The lab report included commentary that exhilarated my heart. It read, "Subject potentially qualifies as an absolute response". I printed the report, grabbed a marker and edited the word potentially. I modified the wording to read "Subject absolutely qualifies as an absolute response." I did this as a declaration of faith. God's love and mercy suddenly overwhelmed me so mightily, I was capable of nothing but weeping in gratitude.

I was excited for my next two rounds of treatments; it was clear a miracle was unfolding in my body and I was driven to share it with everyone. Every time I received a chemo treatment, I had a different infusion nurse. On this next to last round of chemo, we were gifted a nurse who made an impact on us. I chose a window booth that would allow me to stretch out for the infusion. Our nurse smiled, *"I feel the positive energy over here and I know you know what I mean."* She turned to Stephanie and said, *"You should climb up there too and lay with him."*

We sensed she was a Christian and discerned our faith but needed to remain professional. She proceeded to declare without any knowledge of my situation, *"Let's put the magic in and finish this off. Your stockings are already stuffed."*

I was about to close my eyes and enter a place of meditation when she strolled over again and whispered, *"I want you two, to imagine this booth is actually a train ride together. You two are in a private window compartment heading somewhere good. When this is all done I want you to tell me where you guys have arrived."* She gave us a grin and closed the curtain.

Stephanie and I embraced this chance to envision a future. We whispered back and forth what we envisioned. Both of us imagined a future where I was healed. In our future together, we were encouraging and helping others on their journeys. We both expected a future where our hearts were overflowing with love, life, joy, and freedom. During these intimate moments, I became overwhelmed with love for Stephanie and the gift it was to experience life together. I did not share it with her, but I asked GOD for a day where she would get to use her gift of writing and encouragement to its fullest.

November 24, 2017

Thanksgiving Day was here, and I certainly felt gratitude in my heart. Our young adult daughter during this season of her life was living with my parents during the week and us on the weekends. We made these arrangements to accommodate both her needs for work transportation and my need to not absorb stress. The stress stemmed from my ineffective efforts to fix the trajectory of life she was on. She was choosing to jump into dark and evil places with both feet. We picked her up from my parents to join us for a large family dinner on Stephanie's side. When I say large I mean it. The family gathering held at a church reception hall had over a hundred people appreciating dinner and fellowship together.

Throughout dinner, Stephanie and I were engaged in many discussions updating her extended family on our journey. Suddenly I noticed Ashley had not returned to the dining hall for a period of time longer than a normal bathroom visit, even for a girl her age. I asked others if they had seen her and no one had for at least fifteen minutes.

I pulled out my phone and instantly a message came up. The text was from the guy she was seeing. This relationship was very dark and unhealthy, but I will leave those details for another time. The message indicated they had broken up and Ashley was threatening suicide and was presently in hysterics.

I quickly told Stephanie and a few others what I had just learned, and the search began. I went outside and began speed walking around the neighborhood adjacent to the church. I kept trying to call her, but she would not answer calls or text messages. My heart was racing, and I knew this was not mere drama; she was in serious trouble. I called out to GOD asking him to help me find her and keep her safe.

On my tenth call to her while searching, she finally answered. As described, she was completely in hysterics and determined to end her life. I begged her to tell me where she was, but she hung up. During the brief exchange, I heard a train in the background. I knew of train tracks a few blocks away. I did not hesitate even for a moment to update anyone on this new information. Somehow, I knew there was not enough time. I jumped in my car and raced towards the tracks. I came to an intersection running parallel to the railroad. This was a hub of tracks for industry with at least six sets going both directions from the intersection. I decided I must turn left. The tracks were a good fifty yards back from the roadway and it was pitch-black. Occasionally shadows would occur due to lights of businesses on the other side of the tracks. My heart prayed let me catch a glimmer of her.

Suddenly I glimpsed a silhouette of my daughter, she was venturing deeper into the tracks. She longed for one with a train approaching. The next part of this story gets a bit fuzzy in my memory. I arrived at her approaching her back as she was at tracks with a train approaching. I threw my arms around her and dragged her back, *"No way! We love you; no boy is ever worth your life."*

My daughter sobbed and pleaded, *"Just let me do it Dad."* I continued speaking life and love as I escorted her towards the car.

On our way to the car, I realized that somehow even in my post-chemo state I had traversed quite a few hurdles. I had crossed lanes of oncoming traffic, negotiated a ravine and made it past three sets of tracks to reach her. My car was idling along the other side of a four-lane road with the door still hanging open. I called Stephanie and shared, *"Our daughter is alive."* Stephanie spread the news.

We ultimately needed to involve a behavior health commitment but again that is for another time. Our daughter's life was spared. GOD was there for us again. "He said Life!" My heart kept recalling the lyrics to "Reckless Love "and how GOD will leave the ninety-nine to go after the one and there is no shadow he won't light up, no mountain he won't climb up coming after us.

Treasure from
the Darkness

*If you are winning a spiritual battle, keep your eyes open
for collateral damage on vulnerable loved ones.*

Treasure in the Darkness

December 6, 2017

The last scheduled round of chemotherapy was dripping into my body. I called to memory the many amazing things GOD had sorted out on this journey. I focused introspectively on how he changed my heart, affected my family, co-workers and so many others. The ripples of this life-changing event were bearing good fruit. I contemplated how GOD uses all things for the good of those who love him. I searched my heart and I truly believed I was healed, and GOD had plans for my future. I sensed the only thing missing was seeing the clinical reports confirming what my heart knew.

Once this last round was completed our nurse told us, *"We do not have a bell you ring here but I have a little something for you."* He pulled out his phone and a song began to play "Hit the road Jack… don't come back, come back no more."

Our nurse smirked, *"I don't want to see you here again, unless it is to share good news!"*

We chatted a bit more and I assured him, *"I believed that will, in fact, be the case."* I thanked everyone in the infusion room for their help.

Stephanie and I celebrated and praised GOD for carrying us through all my rounds of chemo with only minimal side effects. Because of his grace, we were not only surviving but thriving. We were transforming and growing into improved versions of ourselves.

December 7-11, 2017

Even though my chemo rounds were now completed spiritual dreams continued. GOD was teaching me through many of my dreams. I discerned I was to read Isaiah 45:3. *"I will give you hidden treasures, riches stored in the secret places, so that you may know that I am the Lord the God of Israel, who summons you by name."* My heart raced, and I had an instant revelation of what this meant for me. This scripture was describing exactly what was taking place. GOD was giving me life-changing treasures that were hidden in the darkness. There are treasures in life that can only be found amid trials and struggles. In fact, the kingdom of GOD is described as a treasure hidden.

The lesson GOD was teaching me continued, my devotional reading the next morning elaborated on what GOD had just illuminated in my heart. The devotional author referenced the parable of the pebbles. Apparently, this non-biblical parable has been retold in several different ways but with a similar message.

In the version I will share, three horse riders or knights were on a critical mission from GOD. It was vitally important they reached their destination. It was so important they could not rest, and they continued to ride even through the night. Suddenly without warning, they all perceived GOD command them the exact same thing. "As you cross the upcoming stream get off your horse and pick up pebbles." GOD also allowed them to all perceive that they would be both glad and sad come dawn. The riders obeyed and in haste dismounted briefly picking up several stones each. However, they put little value into this task beyond obedience. Each knight only grabbing a few pebbles. They were driven by their passion to reach the commanded destination. When daylight broke, all three wrestled the pebbles out of their bags while continuing to ride, hoping to understand what the rides interruption was about. It turned out these pebbles gathered in haste were magnificent gems. The lesson of this parable can be easily understood. These knights were pleased with the gems they had been led to but were disappointed they had not gathered more.

GOD was teaching me, in the storms of our life, we can receive some of the most valuable gifts or tools we will ever receive. Instead of only pleading, "GOD please rescue me, get me out of here!" We must learn to find peace, knowing he is the LORD of the storm and in control. We must participate in what he is teaching us and ask to see all the treasures stored for us in the darkness. This revelation has forever changed me. I know GOD's heart even in the worst storm is filled with love and purpose.

Treasure from
the Darkness

There are treasures that can be found nowhere else but in the midst of trials and suffering. Ask not only for a triumph over the trial but for all the hidden treasures.

Tree of Life

December 15-17, 2017

Post-therapy scans were on the calendar. These scans would reveal how effective the treatments had been and what was presently taking place in my body. A getaway for the weekend with our children seemed in order. Our destination was a beach town in the middle of winter. Little did we know GOD had a surprise planned for us.

During one of our weekend strolls on the boardwalk, our future daughter in love had a flash in her memory. What she recalled was there was a hidden geocache box not far from where we were walking. We all followed her as she pulled out a box completely hidden from any non-seeker's eyes. She began to open this hidden treasure chest.

For anyone reading who does not know about geocache boxes, here is a quick 101. They are boxes hidden for scavenger hunters. People use their phones and GPS to locate these hidden boxes. The boxes can be simple containing only a logbook you sign your name on and hide again. The hidden caches can also be larger containers filled with assorted goodies, gifts, gift cards, etc. The idea being, if you take something out, you put something back in and keep the fun going for others.

As this container was being opened we huddled around, wondering what treasures it may contain. On the very top of this box full of goodies lay a wooden token of the tree of life! Both Stephanie and I felt faint from the sheer shock of what we were looking at. This particular tree of life looked like it had been cut right off the cover of my journal. Our daughter in love exclaims, *"I know you guys want that, you can take it you know, you just have to put something back in."* The mad dash starts, searching our bags for an item to replace this obvious gift from GOD. We locate and add a token gift into the box replacing this priceless treasure. The chest is returned to its hiding place awaiting the next seekers.

Unknown to me, Stephanie had just been thinking of my journal, she had taken a picture recently of our hands resting on it and posted it on Facebook declaring a proclamation of life. That very image had just popped into her mind as we were walking. She saw a family getting pictures on the beach and prayed silently, *"That is all I want God. His life, our life together."* As she prayed this image of our hands on the journal came to mind.

We continued walking, overwhelmed by the treasure, our plan to visit a coffee shop. I marveled at the carving I was now holding. I noticed this treasure had a trackable tag attached to it with an ID number and website. The moment we arrived at the coffee shop I searched what this Id tag could tell me about our new treasure. As I reviewed the information on the website, tears rolled down my cheeks. I proceeded to share with everyone what I was reading. This Tree of life token started its journey seven years ago in Slovakia. It had traveled through Finland, France, Italy, Germany, Ireland, and numerous other countries in Europe. In fact, the site tracked this item had traveled more than 17,000 miles and arrived in the very box we discovered it in just days before our arrival. All I can surmise from this, GOD is never surprised by where we are in life. We never take a step or breath outside of his love.

December 18-19, 2017

We arrived again in Baltimore. This time we were in town for post-treatment scans. The many scans and blood labs scheduled would keep us in town for two days. On the first day all the scans would be completed and the second day we would discuss the results with our beloved Dr. Emmanuel.

I made the best of my time in the scanners, singing in my heart and watching for an opportunity to share what GOD was doing in me. It was a long first day, so we returned to our hotel. An email popped up on my phone indicating I had test results uploaded to my online chart. I felt both nervousness and expectant. The CT and bone scans displayed significant improvements. Many prominent lesions from the past, no longer even being mentioned. However, the report still indicated radio-tracer uptake to a large vertebra in my spine. This discouraged me some. *"It is good but not good enough. I need to see nothing at all lighting up."*

We decided no matter what, our trust was in GOD. He did not bring us this far to see us crushed. I considered to myself, perhaps there is more treasure to be found and the journey is not yet complete. We were exhausted, so we laid it before the LORD and fell asleep.

We awoke to a beautiful morning and had a little time before our drive to Hopkins. While getting ready we turned on the television to the 700 Club. They began airing one of their miracle segments where they recreate a video of an amazing story. In this story, a family was told their newborn child would never get to go home with them. The medical team advised at most you have a couple of hours to be together. The entire family was present, and they called on

GOD together asking for healing. Unfortunately, the child continued to deteriorate. The family seemed to be losing zeal in their prayers for healing. The room grew quiet, but the grandfather must have had a revelation of how they should pray. He held the baby and gathered the family to pray again. No longer pleading for healing, he gratefully thanked GOD declaring, *"Thank you Lord for this precious promise and life."* The faith in the room grew, as he thanked GOD that they would be soon bringing this blessing home. Once the prayers transitioned to thanksgiving to GOD the child began to improve, color returned to her body and she was healing. This shocked the medical staff; leaving them with no words but miracle. The story continued showing the child years later playing in her back yard joyfully living life.

I mentioned to Stephanie, *"Perhaps this is for us. We need to thank God for what he has already done in my body and the finished healing that is coming."* We prayed, and tears of thankfulness flowed.

We arrived and parked ourselves in the waiting room, grasping each other's hands a bit tighter than normal. As much as I longed to be at peace I sensed my adrenaline running and my blood pressure heightened. The nurse called my name and escorted us back to the room. As we approached the door of the examination room, Dr. Emmanuel stood up and greeted us with a pleasant smile. He started questioning if they had ever sequenced my cells. I was taken back slightly but said, *"Only the DNA testing that was done."*

"If you're OK with us fully sequencing your cells we should get you to sign off on us doing it."

I agreed. I will never forget the next sentence he spoke. *"OK scans, scans are good. You are heading into remission. In fact, you are already in remission."*

Stephanie and I were shocked to hear this. The scan we looked at the night before showed radio-tracer uptake still to a bone in my spine. I proceeded to ask about what I saw on the scan. Our doctor indicated he believed this was my bone healing. He continued to explain they look at a combination of blood markers, scans and then conclude their prognosis using all the data combined. The conclusion in my case was I was in remission and my body was healing.

Joy. True joy is something I assumed I understood but apparently, I had never felt to this level. My heart leaped as I was finally hearing the doctor confirm what I knew in my heart. GOD had orchestrated a path moved mountains leading to the healing of both my body and soul. On the ride home, Stephanie and I called as many of our family, friends, and supporters as we could to declare the works of the LORD and share the joy.

January 2018

Even with the miraculous news in December, the Hopkins team set us up for another round of scans only a month later. Leading up to the January scans GOD had another loving, unbelievable surprise for me. Since I was having so many spiritual dreams, I felt compelled to seek out a book that might assist me in understanding certain imagery better. I went online and located a book that seemed to be what I was looking for. The price, however, was eighteen dollars. I was not certain I wanted to spend that much for a book I may or may not find value in. I considered the possibility of only reading a few pages of if it and find no value in it. If that happened, it would be eighteen dollars in the trash. I decided to try and find a used copy for sale online. Very quickly I found a used book store in Georgia that had a copy for a mere eighty cents. I immediately ordered it figuring even if I did not like it, I wasted very little.

The book arrived at our home a day before my January scan date. When I came home from work, I opened the package. My first thought was, I wonder if the owner before me underlined any useful statements. I started to flip through the pages and suddenly a postcard fell out of the book onto my living room floor. I picked it up, finding myself in amazement at what I saw. The front of this post-card was the chapter Psalms 91. This was the most precious chapter to me during my journey. In fact, one of our dear prayer warrior friends kept telling me over and over he was declaring Psalms 91 over my life daily.

I stared at it for a moment in disbelief; was GOD encouraging me again that he was in this and that I had a promise of a long life? I turned over the postcard to see who may have happened to be using this as a bookmark. I wondered if I would see someone's name. address and personal message. I flipped over the postcard and could not have fathomed what I was reading. The postcard had a hand-written note that simply read I am expecting a miracle and a miracle is expecting me.

Stephanie called me as I sat in awe. This was a routine on her way home from work. I mumbled to her, *"I believe God has given us another 'God Wink' but I do not want to tell you, I want to show you."* When she arrived home, we marveled in the joy together over this amazing and unexpected gift from GOD.

The day of January scans arrived and somehow in spite of all the favor and love GOD was showering on us we still had to tame our emotions. The scans were completed and once again showed only an undetectable blood marker and additional bone healing. We praised GOD and were excited to hear we would now be moving to a once every three-month scan regimen.

April 2018-present

Prior to our April scans, Stephanie felt in her spirit that GOD had a surprise for her. The scans were great again and the blood marker un-detectable. Our trial nurse declared, *"Good news since you have had three undetectable in a row, we are now switching CT and bone scans to only once a year. You will still need to come every three months for blood work and med-ication refills but no scans."* This was the surprise Stephanie was given.

Since the day our nurse announced the move to once a year scans, I have received reports indicating only undetectable blood work num-bers. The first full-body scans a year out, showed not only that there is no cancer but that my bones that once carried lesions have healed. My medical team is no longer giving us looks of disbelief. They are instead calling me their number one inspirational patient.

The overwhelming storm clouds that surrounded us, have drifted off into the distance. The sun was now shining, and the air smells sweet. Peace and love saturate my heart and mind. We were not de-stroyed, but we were changed. The tempest and GOD's grace refined us. I no longer view life as drudgery, I cherish every breath. My heart and dreams are now enlarged. I have been given a reprieve and sec-ond chance to live a life fully alive.

If you read this book because of your own cancer journey, or that of a loved one, know this. GOD made you and loves you dearly. You do not need to be a giant in the faith to see a victory. What it takes is a genuine reliance on him and obedience. Press in, know him, trust him, give him all you are. Remain in the shadow of the Almighty and do not forget to ask for the treasures in the darkness.

Moving Forward

Moving forward... What now?

Most journeys have a clear beginning but not all have a clear ending point. GOD is now using us to encourage others. I have gone through plant-based cooking courses, nutrition courses and have begun speaking at churches, cancer walks and even medical events. We have been assisting individuals with their cancer journeys, encouraging them to lean into their faith, improve their diets and to look for the treasures in the darkness.

Stephanie and I do not fully know exactly how GOD plans to use us, but we have told GOD we will not say "No". We have a passion to tell others our story and give them hope. We also sense the faith and anointing to pray GOD's healing power over others. I also have a passion to teach about nutrition and living healthier lives. We feel there is more that will come out of the work GOD has done. A secret dream we have is to sell all we have, purchase a Tree of Life branded RV and travel the country, going where he leads and encouraging those that cross our path. Perhaps we will see you in the future.

Also keep your eyes open for my next book covering in detail the nutritional part of my journey.

You can connect with us at www.GodSaidLife.com

About the Author

S hawn Russell is a "Survivor", he is employed as an employee benefits consultant and has a B.S. in Business from Penn State. He is passionate about nutrition, travel, and faith. *They Said Terminal: God Said Life* is his debut title as an author. Shawn and his wife Stephanie live in south-central Pennsylvania and share their life changing experiences with many audiences.

CPSIA information can be obtained
at www.ICGtesting.com
Printed in the USA
BVHW032353190719
553982BV00001B/9/P